SCIENCE JUMPSTARTERS!

*175 Ready-to-Use Earth,
Life & Physical Science
Activities for Grades 6-12*

ROBERT G. HOEHN

**THE CENTER FOR APPLIED
RESEARCH IN EDUCATION**
Paramus, New Jersey 07652

Library of Congress Cataloging-in-Publication Data

Hoehn, Robert G.
    Science jumpstarters! : 175 ready-to-use earth, life & physical science
activities for grades 6-12 / Robert G. Hoehn.
      p. cm.
    ISBN 0-13-028424-6
    1. Science—Study and teaching—Activity programs. I. Title.

Q181 .H715 2001
507'.1—dc21   00-050852

©2001 by The Center for Applied Research in Education

Acquisitions Editor: *Connie Kallback*
Production Editor: *Tom Curtin*
Interior Design/Formatting: *Robyn Beckerman*

Printed in the United States of America

10 9 8 7 6 5 4 3 2 1

ISBN 0-13-028424-6

**THE CENTER FOR APPLIED RESEARCH
IN EDUCATION**
Paramus, NJ 07652

http://www.phdirect.com

DEDICATION
To Ona Castaneda for continual support and friendship.

ABOUT THE AUTHOR

Robert G. Hoehn has taught earth science, physical science, and biology in the Roseville Joint Union High School District of California since 1963. He has received seven National Summer Science grants from the National Science Foundation and has given numerous presentations to teachers and administrators attending local and state science conventions, workshops, and seminars. He has also served as a mentor teacher in his district.

Mr. Hoehn has a B.A. from San Jose State University and an administration credential from California State University, Sacramento. He is a member of the National Education Association, California Teacher's Association, and California Science Teacher's Association. Author of *Science Puzzlers!,* 1995, and other science resources for teachers by The Center for Applied Research in Education, he has also published a number of nonfiction books and over 70 magazine articles on science education and coaching.

ABOUT THIS RESOURCE

What eight-letter word spells relief for today's busy science educator? The answer, of course, is resource.

Science Jumpstarters! is a handy resource loaded with 175 ready-to-go activities.

This resource provides the following outstanding features:

- It covers the three major science areas—earth, life, and physical science—commonly taught in elementary, middle school, and high school.

- The single-page format provides a mix of puzzlers, problem solvers, and thought provokers—all designed to help students strengthen their thinking skills while reviewing important science concepts. These activities get the class going and immediately engage students in the day's work.

- Each single-page activity can be completed in 20 minutes or less, thus providing an excellent closing assignment for students. These activities are tailored to rev up the thinking process, encourage students to ask questions, and stimulate classroom discussion.

- Humor weaves its way throughout various activities. Youngsters tend to take an active role in their learning when FUN creeps into the curriculum. Several of the activities allow students to tackle science concepts in a playful manner.

Science Jumpstarters! offers an appealing menu of activities for students, grades 6 through 12. It provides a fresh approach to an old problem: How do you grab and hold a student's attention during tough teaching moments?

You have 175 science activities at your disposal. You may use them as regular classwork, supplemental activities during class, for outside assignments, and for extra-credit projects.

Each single-page assignment can be easily reproduced and made available to every student.

A complete Answer Key, found at the end of the book, can be kept for your own use or made available to students for self study.

Science Jumpstarters! will supply you with a diversity of activities to promote thinking and stimulate learning. Select the ones you feel have the best chance of motivating your students and meet the needs of your current lessons.

Robert G. Hoehn
Independence High School
Roseville, CA

CONTENTS

Part I
Earth Science

Part II
Life Science

Part III
Physical Science

Answer Key 187

Part I

Earth Science

ES-1
Earth Scientists

Fill in the blanks with the area of study for each of the following scientists. Then darken the letters in the puzzle that spell the names of each study area. Answers are listed from left to right in the puzzle.

1. A geologist studies the _ _ _ _ _.
2. A seismologist studies _ _ _ _ _ _ _ _ _ _ _.
3. A cartographer studies _ _ _ _.
4. A stratigrapher studies the Earth's rock _ _ _ _ _ _.
5. A limnologist studies lakes and _ _ _ _ _.
6. An astronomer studies the _ _ _ _ _ _ _ _ _.
7. A tectonophysicist studies the Earth's _ _ _ _ _ and _ _ _ _ _ _ _ that shape the Earth.
8. An archaeologist studies ancient _ _ _ _ _ _ and _ _ _ _ _ _ _ _ _ _ _.
9. A petrologist studies _ _ _ _ _ _.
10. A paleontologist studies the preserved evidence of _ _ _ _ _ _ _ _ _ (2 words).

P	A	S	T	L	I	F	E	T	U	N	I
V	E	R	S	E	L	A	Y	E	R	S	O
M	A	P	S	P	O	N	D	S	I	C	I
T	I	E	S	A	R	T	I	F	A	C	T
S	R	C	R	U	S	T	F	O	R	C	E
S	E	A	R	T	H	Q	U	A	K	E	S
R	R	O	C	K	S	E	A	R	T	H	S

Bonus Challenge: Use five of the unshaded letters in the puzzle to complete the answer to this question:

What do you call a person who studies the waters of the earth?

Answer: The person is called a h y d _ _ l o g _ _ _.

ES–2
Here on Earth, Part 1

What do these mean?   <u>man</u>   and   <u>the microscope</u>
                     board   specimen

They refer to "man overboard" and "specimen under the microscope." How about trying 10 more related to earth science? Match Column A (over, above, or under items) with their meanings in Column B. Place the letter from Column B in the space next to Column A.

Column A

____	1.	<u>ground</u> water
____	2.	<u>point</u> focus of earthquake
____	3.	<u>wind</u> water
____	4.	<u>stress</u> rock bends
____	5.	<u>sedimentary rock</u> sedimentary rock
____	6.	<u>tow</u> strong
____	7.	<u>pressure</u> rocks
____	8.	<u>water</u> landslides
____	9.	<u>stalactites</u> stalagmites
____	10.	<u>trapped infrared rays</u> Earth's surface

Column B

a. calcite deposits

b. rip or bottom current

c. stratification

d. epicenter

e. may cause tsunami

f. source of fresh water

g. folding

h. stretched and squeezed

i. creates waves

j. greenhouse effect

Name _____ Date _____

ES–3
Here on Earth, Part 2

How about solving 10 more over, above, or under items related to earth science? As you did in Part 1, match Column A items with their meanings in Column B. Place the letter from Column B in the space next to Column A.

Column A

_____ 1. $\dfrac{\text{ultraviolet light}}{\text{glows}}$

_____ 2. $\dfrac{\text{Earth's crust}}{\text{rock}}$

_____ 3. $\dfrac{\text{the sea}}{\text{life}}$

_____ 4. $\dfrac{\text{change of organisms}}{\text{time}}$

_____ 5. $\dfrac{\text{surface soil}}{\text{frozen subsoil}}$

_____ 6. $\dfrac{\text{pressure}}{\text{carbon}}$

_____ 7. $\dfrac{\text{height}}{\text{sea level}}$

_____ 8. $\dfrac{\text{lithosphere}}{\text{asthenosphere}}$

_____ 9. $\dfrac{\text{weather conditions}}{\text{many years}}$

_____ 10. $\dfrac{\text{change in elevation}}{\text{a distance}}$

Column B

a. gradient

b. mantle

c. coral, fish, etc.

d. related to plate tectonics

e. climate

f. altitude

g. fluorescence

h. evolution

i. may produce a diamond

j. tundra

ES–4
Earth Happenings

Use your knowledge of Earth's features, products, and events to help you identify each item below. The clue words are related in some way to the answer.

1. Heavy rain or fiery glow
   Creates this icky, sticky dough.
   Clue Words: rapid movement, soil and rocks
   The event is a _____.

2. Wind, water, and moving ice
   Make the rocks tumble nice.
   Clue Words: earth materials, redeposited
   The event is _____.

3. Energy waves, no hocus-pocus
   Underground rocks will be the focus.
   Clue Words: fracture, magnitude
   The event is an _____.

4. Once a river flowing red
   Now considered mostly dead.
   Clue Words: igneous, inactive
   The feature is a _____ _____.

5. There's not much room for scattered rocks
   To move around in huge ice blocks.
   Clue Words: glacial melting, deposits
   The feature is a _____.

6. Once alive and doing well
   Now an outline of a shell.
   Clue Words: evidence, past life
   The product is a _____.

7. Rooftop spikes of calcite fame
   Boasts of limestone just the same.
   Clue Words: caves, icicles
   The feature is a _____.

8. Ocean earthquake deep below
   Sends a wall of H_2O.
   Clue Words: gigantic; long, low waves
   The event is a _____.

Name _____ Date _____

ES–5
Mapping

1. Four of the statements below are false. Circle the letter preceding each false statement.

   a. A flat map shows distortion due to the curvature of the earth.

   b. As you look at a map, the left is east.

   c. A topographic map shows the changes in elevation of the earth's surface.

   d. Maps drawn on a flat piece of paper show accurate crustal features.

   e. Contour lines on a map show changes in elevation.

   f. A mercator map projection shows the Mercator Islands in three dimensions.

   g. Relief or irregularity in elevation of parts of the earth's' surface is easy to show on a map.

2. These map symbols are incomplete. Complete them by drawing in the missing parts.

   a.
   depression

   b. [filled square]
   church

   c. [filled rectangle]
   school

   d.
   trail, Point a to Point b

   e.
   hilltop, elevation 920'

   f.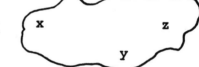
   railroad connecting points x, y, and z

   g.
   4 buildings, south east area

3. The west side of Cobra Island is steep. Show, using five or six contour lines, how this might appear on a topographic map.

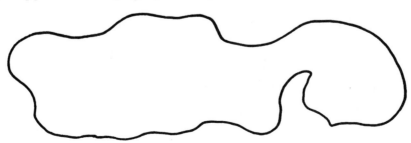

ES–6
Space Objects

Planets and moons orbit the sun. So do other space objects like comets, meteors, and asteroids. Let's investigate further.

1. *It's a Gas*: Use four of the following terms to complete the statement: ground, dust, planet, liquid, rock, gases, solar, frozen

   A comet is a mass of _____ _____, _____ and

   small _____ particles that travels around the sun.

2. *X or Y?*: Which of the two comets, X or Y, would you more likely see from Earth? Give a reason for your answer.

   ○   ●   •
   Sun   Earth   Comet X

   ○   ●   •
   Sun   Earth   Comet Y

   I'd more likely see Comet _____ because _____

   _____.

3. *Meteoroid, Meteor, Meteorite*: Use each of the three words in this title to complete the following descriptions.

   a. A _____ is a solid body traveling through outer space.

   b. A _____ is a solid body traveling through outer space that burns up in Earth's atmosphere.

   c. A _____ is a solid body that penetrates the earth's atmosphere and strikes the earth's surface.

4. *Space Rocks*: Asteroids are rock fragments that orbit the sun. They range in size from less than one km to over 1,000 km in diameter. Use the clues to complete the words that reveal things about asteroids.

   Asteroid's other names: _ _ a _ _ _ _; Belongs to this system: s _ _ _ _; Known as a minor _ _ _ _ _ _ t; Region of many asteroids: _ e _ _; Moves around sun: _ r _ _ _ _; Solid part of asteroid: _ o _ _; Asteroid ingredient: i _ _ _; Ceres has the largest of these: d _ _ _ _ _ _ _ _.

Name _____   Date _____

ES–7
Sun Time

The sun (sol), our nearest star, is about 93 million miles from Earth. Without this "sol provider," we would cease to exist. Place answers to each item below in the empty spaces. Then fill in the puzzle blanks with the letters from each answer. Answers may be up, down, backward, or forward. Use the letter clues in the puzzle to help you.

1. When should you look into the sun? __ __ __ __ __

2. The sun produces this. __ __ __ __ __ __ __

3. The fourth planet from the sun. __ __ __ __

4. The sun is one. __ __ __ __

5. The sun has a 864,000-mile __ __ __ __ __ __ __ __ __.

6. One of the sun's gases. __ __ __ __ __ __ __ __ __

7. The sun's light has a __ __ __ __ __ __ __ __ __ of 186,000 miles per second.

8. The sun can create this warm, moist condition. __ __ __ __ __ __

9. This term means "under the influence of the sun." __ __ __ __ __ __

10. The dark surface areas of the sun are sun__ __ __ __ __.

11. These are beams of light from the sun. __ __ __ __

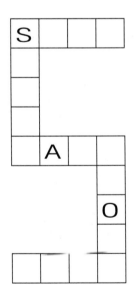 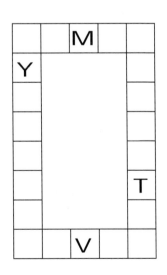 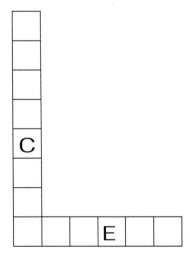

Riddle: What do you call a group of astronomers called together to discuss the sun?

Answer: They are called a _____.

ES–8
Moon Things

Complete the crossword puzzle using information you know (or can find) about the moon.

ACROSS

2. We see the moon by reflected _____.
3. These are saucer-like depressions on the moon's surface.
5. A name for trench-like areas on the moon's surface.
8. Dark areas on the surface of the moon.
9. We see different phases of the moon as the moon _____ around Earth.
11. A large, well-known moon crater.
13. These things are known to have battered the moon.

DOWN

1. This term means reflected light.
4. A term for the moon as it relates to the earth.
6. A lunar _____ occurs when Earth comes between the moon and the sun.
7. The point in orbit where the moon is closest to Earth.
10. The moon cannot _____ life.
12. The surface gravity of the moon is about one-_____ the surface gravity of Earth's.

© 2001 by The Center for Applied Research in Education

ES–9
Planet Mercury

1. Mercury, the innermost planet, is approximately 36 million miles from the sun. The earth in the diagram below is 93 million miles from the sun. Let one centimeter equal 10 million miles. Place an X between Earth and the sun to show Mercury's distance from the sun.

●
Sun
                                                                 Earth

2. Why do you think the Romans named the first planet from the sun Mercury? HINT: Mercurius was the messenger of the gods in Roman mythology.

3. Two "No-No's" prevail on Mercury. What are they? The answers are broken down into paired letters scattered in the box below. Unscramble the paired letters and place the answers in the blanks.

mo	re	sp	on	he	at	mo

Mercury does not have a _ _ _ _ _ or _ _ _ _ _ _ _ _ _ _ _ _.

4. The underlined word is scrambled in each of the following statements. Write the unscrambled word in the space to the left of the statement.

_____ a. The surface temperature of Mercury is hot enough to melt <u>dela.</u>

_____ b. Mercury has a weak <u>gicmaten</u> field.

_____ c. Mercury's surface is covered with <u>rcaerts.</u>

_____ d. Mercury <u>rtbios</u> the sun in 88 days.

_____ e. Mercury is known as a <u>realsteritr</u> planet.

5. Craters on Mercury hold names for authors, composers, and artists. For example, craters have been named after Bach, Tolstoy, Renoir, Beethoven, and Michelangelo. If you could give names to three craters on a newly discovered planet, what would they be?

_____

_____

6. *Planet Puzzler:* Why do Mercury and the sun have a good relationship?

_____

_____

ES–10
Planet Venus

1. Venus is approximately 67 million miles from the sun. Earth in the diagram is 93 million miles from the sun. Let one centimeter equal 10 million miles. Place an X between Earth and the sun to show Venus's distance from the sun.

●
Sun

●
Earth

2. Fill in the blanks with answers scattered across the face of Venus. Answers may be upside down, forward, or backward.

a. Venus goes through _ _ _ _ _ _.
b. Trapped heat on Venus's surface produces the "_ _ _ _ _ _ _ _ _ _ effect."
c. Venus's atmosphere contains 96-percent carbon _ _ _ _ _ _ _.
d. Venus has no _ _ _ _ _.
e. Venus has no _ _ _ _ _ in its atmosphere.

3. The surface of Venus shows mountains, volcanoes, and lava plains. Sketch a continuing profile from Point A to Point B of these features in the space below.

A_____B

4. Venus is the second closest planet to the sun. If Venus is a planet, why do you think it's called the evening and morning star?

_____

_____

_____

5. *Planet Puzzler:* Use three circles to show where carbon dioxide may be found in Venus's C L O U D Y   A T M O S P H E R E.

Name _____   Date _____

ES–11
Planet Earth

1. Here is a mini-quiz about Earth. Let's see if you can get 8 or more items correct. Place the letter matching the correct answer in the space to the left of each item.

____ a. The earth's atmosphere contains mostly: (a) oxygen (b) hydrogen (c) carbon dioxide (d) nitrogen.

____ b. The earth's shape resembles a (an): (a) perfect circle (b) pear (c) oblate rectangle (d) oblate spheroid.

____ c. A term used for solid earth: (a) ecology (b) geosphere (c) hydrosphere (d) exosphere.

____ d. Scientists study the earth's interior using: (a) direct methods (b) hydro equipment (c) indirect methods (d) surveying equipment.

____ e. The earth's mantle lies: (a) on the surface of the earth (b) between the crust and the inner core (c) between the outer core and inner core (d) between the crust and outer core.

____ f. Sandstone and shale are examples of: (a) sedimentary rock (b) igneous rock (c) metamorphic rock (d) minerals.

____ g. Which of the following is NOT a fossil fuel? (a) coal (b) electricity (c) natural gas (d) petroleum

____ h. According to geologic history, what landmass existed about 200 million years ago? (a) Tethys (b) Primordia (c) Pangaea (d) Lithosland

____ i. Salty ocean water is composed mostly of a: (a) chlorine (b) salt (c) magnesium (d) water.

____ j. Most fossils are found in: (a) igneous rock (b) sedimentary rock (c) tar pools (d) amber deposits.

2. Use the clues to identify features on Earth.

		Clues
_ _ _ E _ _ _		basic crustal material
_ _ A _ _ _ _		mass of moving ice
R _ _ _		collection of minerals
T _ _ _ _ _		deep valley in ocean floor
_ _ _ _ H _ _		atmospheric condition

3. The earth holds many surprises, including a puzzle or two. These five puzzlers will challenge your creative thinking power.

   a. Why is Earth's crust falling apart?

   b. Why will the earth NEVER be perfect?

   c. What makes up 100 percent of Earth?

   d. What part of an earthquake does the LEAST amount of damage?

   e. Where would the earth be without the sun?

ES–12
Planet Mars

1. Circle the letters in the puzzle that spell the answers to each item. The circled letters will reveal the answer to the bonus item. Answers may be up, down, forward, or backward.

   a. The visual impression of a planet sent to Earth from a spacecraft. __ __ __ __ __

   b. Two of these orbit Mars. __ __ __ __ __

   c. What an instrumental spacecraft does. __ __ __ __ __ __

   d. The path of Mars around the sun. __ __ __ __ __

   e. The sister moon of Deimos, a Martian moon. __ __ __ __ __ __

   f. This comes from Martian volcanoes. __ __ __ __

   g. The god of war; identified with the Roman Mars. __ __ __ __

   h. Small amounts of water on Mars are trapped in __ __ __ __ __ ice caps.

```
A
R K X P
E F Z R Y C W M O O N S J P U Z I
S O B O H P D X C R F U D O X F M
U Y J B W F Y   U B K N W L A V A
      E Q       D I J   F A Y J G
      S Z       W T Z   K R U X E
```

Bonus Item: Mars, the red planet, lies between Earth and Jupiter. It is the _____ planet from the sun.

2. Circle SIX features or events from the following items that are known to exist on Mars:

valleys	tsunamis	winds
life	rings	polar caps
dust	seasons	"canals"
carbon dioxide	bacteria	rivers
vegetation	lichen	glaciers

3. In 1976, Viking 1 and Viking 2 spacecrafts took about 4,500 pictures and performed tests on Mars. What did the pictures and tests show? Unscramble the following words and you'll discover four things.

   nkip   syk   on   vginli   srmosigna

   ____ ___   __ _____ _____

   rsock   rawte   rvopa

   _____   _____ _____

© 2001 by The Center for Applied Research in Education

ES–13
Planet Jupiter

1. The answers to the following items about Jupiter are located in the series of letters under each statement.

   a. What do scientists believe cause the Great Red Spot?
      They say it's created by _____.

      densematterhotmaterialammoniamethaneelements

   b. Scientists believe the Great Red Spot is a _____.

      watervaporballhotlavamagneticfieldstormcrater

   c. Jupiter is the _____ planet from the sun.

      secondfourthfifthsixthseventhninthtenth

   d. Jupiter's orbit period is almost _____ years.

      eightnineteneleventwelvethirteenfourteen

   e. Hydrogen makes about _____ % of Jupiter's atmosphere.

      2041536872757881848687889095969798991 00

   f. Three words best describe Jupiter: _____.

      hunkofironballofgasvolcanoeseruptingeverywhere

   g. Jupiter is known to have at least _____ moons.

      two4six8nineteneleven12thirteen1416zero

   h. The largest moons of Jupiter are Ganymede, Callisto, _____,
      and _____.

      IoTritonEuropaAsianaTychoBenGayRoloVoyager

2. Planet diameters (miles): Mercury—3,008; Venus—7,700; Earth—7,900; Mars—4,215; Jupiter—86,800; Saturn—71,500; Uranus—31,700; Neptune—31,000; Pluto—1,430.

   Use the diameter data to answer the following questions:

   a. Would the diameters of Neptune, Venus, Earth, Mars, and Uranus combined be longer than Jupiter's diameter? Circle one: YES   NO

   b. Would the diameters of Saturn, Venus, and Earth combined be longer than Jupiter's diameter? Circle one: YES   NO

   c. Would the diameters of Venus, Mars, and Saturn combined be longer than Jupiter's diameter? Circle one: YES   NO

3. *Bonus Item:* How many Pluto diameters combined would it take to fit inside the diameter of Jupiter? _____

4. *Planet Riddle:* Where would you find a hole or cavity in Jupiter? _____

ES–14
Planet Saturn

1. The answers to the seven items located below can be found in the puzzle. They may be up, down, forward, backward, or diagonal. Circle the answer in the puzzle. Then write the answer on the line.

h	o	t	t	e	r	c	i
u	e	s	n	e	d	o	y
d	o	a	e	w	i	l	t
n	s	l	w	h	v	d	n
o	g	e	t	o	i	e	e
c	n	x	u	a	s	r	w
e	i	a	d	r	i	h	t
s	r	w	e	t	o	i	a
a	s	e	v	e	n	t	h

   a. Saturn is the _____ planet from the sun.
   b. Saturn is the _____ largest planet in our solar system.
   c. Saturn has at least _____ moons.
   d. Saturn has a _____ temperature than Jupiter.
   e. The outer gap in the rings of Saturn is known as the Cassini _____.
   f. Saturn is the least _____ planet in our solar system.
   g. Several _____ surround Saturn.

2. What are Saturn's rings made of? Some scientists believe the rings are numerous smaller particles or circle-like objects known as ringlets. They theorize the ringlets are _____-covered _____ particles. The particles may be as small as a grain of _____. Some may be as large as a _____. Fill in the empty spaces with the correct answers from the following terms.

sedimentary	grain	tree
ice	rock	magma
sugar	canyon	house
lava	tire	carbon

3. Saturn's atmosphere is thought to contain H, He, NH_3, and CH_4. Find and circle the names of the gases in the box below that match these chemical symbols or formulas.

carbon dioxide	nitrogen oxide
hexagon	ammonia
methane	heptane
hydrogen	helium
helio-octane	carbon monoxide

ES–15
Planet Uranus

1. Match the items in Column A with those in Column B. Place the answers from Column B in the spaces to the left of Column A.

Column A

_____ a.   Present on a Uranus moon

_____ b.   Sent images to Earth

_____ c.   Causes blue-green color

_____ d.   Orbit period

_____ e.   One of nine

_____ f.   Miles in diameter

_____ g.   Makes up most of atmosphere

_____ h.   Surrounds Uranus

Column B

1.   62 years
2.   methane gas
3.   rings
4.   32,400 miles
5.   hydrogen gas
6.   Triton
7.   planets
8.   craters
9.   Voyager 2
10. 35,000 miles
11. 84 years
12. carbon dioxide

2. Use the scattered letters below to spell the name of three gases believed to be in Uranus's atmosphere.

```
    h   m                 i           l           o
 e       g       d   h   e       n   t   r               h
     a           m       y           e           u       n   e
```

The gases are _____, _____, and

_____.

3. *Planet Puzzler:* Fifteen minutes after P.E. class started, Mr. Moon, teacher, shouted at the class, "Hey, why are you guys huffing and puffing?" They countered with a one-word response. What was it? HINT: What planet lies between Saturn and Neptune?

The class yelled back, "_____."

4. *Another Planet Puzzler:* How is it possible for MERCURY and NEPTUNE to appear to be the same size as JUPITER?

5. *Still Another Planet Puzzler:* Create a way to write Uranus from the following symbol and three letters:

   U   a   r

ES–16
Planet Neptune

1. Indicate by circling the letter before each item which of the statements are TRUE.

    a. Neptune is the third largest planet in the solar system.

    b. It takes Neptune about 165 years to revolve around the sun.

    c. Neptune may be seen with the naked eye.

    d. Hydrogen, helium, and methane are believed to be in Neptune's atmosphere.

    e. Neptune has a mean density of 1.2.

    f. Neptune was discovered in 1846. It has completed one-and-a-half orbits around the sun since its discovery.

    g. There is a storm-driven Great Dark Spot on Neptune's surface.

    h. Only two moons orbit Neptune: Triton and Nereid. Nereid is the larger of the two.

    i. Neptune may have a rocky core under its gaseous atmosphere.

    j. Neptune is located between Uranus and Pluto.

    k. The name Neptune refers to the Roman god of volcanoes.

2. The upper atmosphere of Neptune is believed to consist of an extremely cold gas. This gas has a molecular make up of carbon and hydrogen. Its name rhymes with insane. Use these clues to complete this sentence: The upper atmosphere of Neptune may be composed of _ _ _ _ _ _   _ _ _ _ _ _ _ gas.

3. Neptune has a diameter about 3.8 times that of Earth. Draw a line 1.5 inches (3 cm) over Point A. This will represent Earth's diameter. Now draw a line over Point B to show how Neptune's diameter compares with Earth's.

        Point A   **Point B**

4. *Planet Puzzler:* Use 16 letters to show how Neptune would look through a telescope.

ES–17
Planet Pluto

Pluto, the smallest and farthest planet from the sun, takes nearly 250 years to orbit the sun. Points 1, 2, 3, and 4 on the diagram represent time intervals on Pluto's orbit. Use the data from the Life Span chart to write the letter and name of the organism on the diagram. This will show how the organism's life span compares to Pluto's revolution around the sun. The first one is done for you.

Life Span

Organism	Years
a. horse	25
b. whale	50
c. carp (fish)	30
d. cat	14
e. tortoise	132
f. human	83
g. guppy (fish)	5
h. elephant	70
i. parrot	60
j. redwood tree	210
k. dog	18

Pluto's Orbit
(0 years)
1

a. horse

(187.5 years)   **4**

2   (62.5 years)

3
(125 years)

Pluto Puzzler: What does this tell you about Pluto? $\dfrac{\text{world}}{\text{god}}$

ES–18
We Need the Water

The water cycle may be described as a constant movement of water from the air to the earth and back again.

1. *Get Wet*: Water occurs throughout Earth in various places. Circle the letters below that spell the names of 11 earth features known to be associated with water.

moleculeoceanfissureswampcreekhorizon
ellipsespringcoronageysercratonpumice
lakeamberumbrarivertravertineaquifera
refractiondamregolithoxidationzoneion
laveaqueductepicenterglaciermagnitude

2. *Cycle Up*: Here's a brief description of the water cycle: The sun's heat causes water to evaporate. Water from plants also enters the atmosphere. This is called transpiration. The water from evaporation and transpiration rises, expands, and slowly cools. Water may condense (change from vapor to liquid) and form clouds. Under the right conditions, water may fall to the earth as precipitation from these clouds. Rain, snow, hail, and sleet are forms of precipitation. The cycle, of course, repeats itself.

Problem: Use this information to explain to a nine-year-old child how the water cycle works. *Challenge:* You may only use the words and symbols in the box for your explanation. You must also keep your explanation to four steps. Use as many arrows as you wish.

The water cycle works like this:

Step 1: _____

Step 2: _____

Step 3: _____

Step 4: _____

ES-19
Earth's Atmosphere

1. Several different gases are found in Earth's atmosphere. Two gases—nitrogen and oxygen—compose the highest percentage of chemicals in the atmosphere. Nitrogen makes up about 78 percent of the atmosphere; oxygen makes up approximately 21 percent. *Problem:* The box below represents Earth's atmosphere. Fill in the spaces with N's (nitrogen) and O's (oxygen) to show the approximate percentage of each element in Earth's atmosphere.

It will take _____ (number of spaces) N's

It will take _____ (number of spaces) O's

2. Many things are related in some way to Earth's atmosphere. Give two examples for EACH letter in the word ATMOSPHERE. The first one is done for you.

A   air, argon, acid rain, aurora borealis _____

T   _____

M   _____

O   _____

S   _____

P   _____

H   _____

E   _____

R   _____

E   _____

3. Circle the numbers next to the two words or phrases that relate to each layer of the atmosphere.

   a. TROPOSPHERE: 1. tropopause, 2. contains 20% carbon dioxide, 3. no water vapor present, 4. weather occurs

   b. STRATOSPHERE: 1. closest to Earth, 2. almost no air movement, 3. dry, cold, thin air, 4. next to exosphere

   c. MESOSPHERE: 1. extremely high temperature, 2. ozone layer, 3. zone of indefinite altitude, 4. extends 300 miles above Earth

   d. THERMOSPHERE: 1. produces ions, 2. air pollution exists, 3. temperature increases steadily with altitude, 4. contains 12% oxygen

ES–20
Weather Instruments Coded Message

Each term below has the same code as the secret message. Fill in the letters for each term and reveal the coded message.

1. __ __ __ __ __ __ __ __ __ __ __ __
   5 18 15 11 8 9 22 14 3 10 3 9
   measures relative humidity

2. __ __ __ __ __ __ __ __ __
   16 4 9 22 14 3 10 3 9
   measures atmospheric pressure

3. __ __ __ __ __ __ __ __ __ __ __
   10 8 3 9 14 22 14 3 10 3 9
   measures air temperature

4. __ __ __ __ __ __ __ __ __ __
   4 25 3 14 22 14 3 10 3 9
   measures wind speed

5. __ __ __ __ __ __ __ __ __
   4 1 10 24 14 3 10 3 9
   measures altitude

6. __ __ __ __ __ __ __ __ __
   14 3 9 11 12 9 24 4 1
   a barometer with mercury

7. __ __ __ __ __ __ __ __ __ __ __
   10 8 3 9 14 22 13 9 4 5 8
   a recording thermometer

8. __ __ __ __ __ __ __ __ __ __
   8 15 13 9 22 14 3 10 3 9
   measures humidity

(continued)

ES–20 (continued)

9. $\underline{\hphantom{x}}$ $\underline{\hphantom{x}}$ $\underline{\hphantom{x}}$ $\underline{\hphantom{x}}$ $\underline{\hphantom{x}}$ $\underline{\hphantom{x}}$ $\underline{\hphantom{x}}$ $\underline{\hphantom{x}}$ $\underline{\hphantom{x}}$
   16   4   9   22   13   9   4   5   8
graphs air-pressure readings

10. $\underline{\hphantom{x}}$ $\underline{\hphantom{x}}$ $\underline{\hphantom{x}}$ $\underline{\hphantom{x}}$ $\underline{\hphantom{x}}$ $\underline{\hphantom{x}}$ $\underline{\hphantom{x}}$ $\underline{\hphantom{x}}$ $\underline{\hphantom{x}}$ (2 words)
   9   4   24   25   13   4   12   13   3
measures precipitation

SECRET MESSAGE: $\underline{\hphantom{x}}$ $\underline{\hphantom{x}}$ $\underline{\hphantom{x}}$ $\underline{\hphantom{x}}$, $\underline{\hphantom{x}}$ $\underline{\hphantom{x}}$ $\underline{\hphantom{x}}$ w,
                         9   4   24   25   18   25   22

$\underline{\hphantom{x}}$ $\underline{\hphantom{x}}$ $\underline{\hphantom{x}}$ $\underline{\hphantom{x}}$, and $\underline{\hphantom{x}}$ $\underline{\hphantom{x}}$ $\underline{\hphantom{x}}$ $\underline{\hphantom{x}}$ $\underline{\hphantom{x}}$ are forms
8   4   24   1   18   1   3   3   10

of $\underline{\hphantom{x}}$ $\underline{\hphantom{x}}$ $\underline{\hphantom{x}}$ $\underline{\hphantom{x}}$ $\underline{\hphantom{x}}$ $\underline{\hphantom{x}}$ $\underline{\hphantom{x}}$ $\underline{\hphantom{x}}$ $\underline{\hphantom{x}}$ $\underline{\hphantom{x}}$ $\underline{\hphantom{x}}$ $\underline{\hphantom{x}}$ $\underline{\hphantom{x}}$.
    5   9   3   11   24   5   24   10   4   10   24   22   25

Weather Whizzer: A hurricane has an eye. How many "eyes" do rain, snow, hail, and sleet have?

Answer: They have _____ "eyes."

ES–21
Air Masses and Fronts

Complete the statements below with the mixed paired words and single jumbled term. You'll need to unscramble the jumbled term and place the paired words and term in their correct order.

		Mixed Words	Jumbled Term
1.	An air mass may extend for _____.	miles of	usnohastd
2.	An air mass has uniform _____.	moisture and	utpreaemrte
3.	A air mass gets its name from the _____.	of place	girnio
4.	An air mass over the sea _____.	much holds	uisomert
5.	A continental arctic air mass is _____.	and cold	dyr
6.	A maritime tropical air mass is _____.	and warm	hduim
7.	The term maritime refers _____.	the to	ecnoa
8.	A polar air mass moving _____.	warmer gets	uhots
9.	A continental air mass _____.	land over	fmosr
10.	A front is the separation of two _____.	masses air	nfdfetire

(continued)

ES–21 (continued)

	Mixed Words	Jumbled Term
11. A front forms when two contrasting _____.	masses air	olecild
12. A warm front with moist air may _____.	violent produce	erhawte
13. A stationary front is one that _____.	move not	sode
14. A warm front occurs when a warm air mass overtakes a _____.	air cold	sams
15. An approaching front means a change _____.	the in	eetarwh
16. Cold air displaces warm air in _____.	cold a	rtofn
17. Warm fronts may bring snow _____.	rain and	yeatsd
18. Thunderstorms may occur at _____.	front a	dloc

ES–22
Clouds

Clouds are tiny masses of condensed water droplets suspended in the atmosphere.

1. *Frustrated Cloud*

I'm a fluff of a cloud
Surely happy and proud
To be drifting from border to border.
But for crying out loud
How good is my shroud,
If you can't put my steps in order?

Therein lies the challenge: You need to put the following steps for cloud development in their proper order. Write Step One in Space A, Step Two in Space B, and so on.

Jumbled Steps: Moist air condenses on dust particles; Air mass expands as it moves upward; The sun's heat causes water to evaporate; Large area of water; Condensed water droplets form clouds; Water vapor rises into the atmosphere; Moist air cools below its dew point.

A. _____

B. _____

C. _____

D. _____

E. _____

F. _____

G. _____

2. *Cloud Typing:* There are three main types of clouds. A cloud's shape and height above the earth's surface determines its classification. Use the letters that spell CLAIM and RUST to identify the following cloud types. You may use a letter more than once.

   a. *Shape:* forms in layers; *Altitude:* low to the ground.

      Cloud Type: __ __ __ __ __ __ __

   b. *Shape:* fluffy, puffy, billowy; *Altitude:* 6,500 feet to 20,000 feet.

      Cloud Type: __ __ __ __ __ __ __

   c. *Shape:* thin, feathery; *Altitude:* 20,000 or higher.

      Cloud Type: __ __ __ __ __ __

Name _____   Date _____

ES–23
Tornadoes and Hurricanes

Tornadoes and hurricanes often create weather conditions that produce devastating results. Let's examine these two atmospheric marvels.

1. *Known as Twister*: Tornadoes are small, destructive storms. Three of the six statements below are true, three are false. The answers to the three math problems that match the numbers in parentheses will give you the correct statements. Write the correct statements in the spaces under the math problems.

    (2/3)   A tornado forms over forests and mountains.

    (24.02)   A tornado may occur on a hot, humid day.

    (6⅔)   The life span of a tornado may last from two to three hours.

    (3/4)   The air pressure of a tornado is much lower than normal atmospheric pressure.

    (22.06)   The air pressure of a tornado is much higher than normal atmospheric pressure.

    (6⅛)   Winds spinning within a tornado's funnel may reach 500 or more miles per hour.

$$2\tfrac{1}{2} + 3\tfrac{2}{3} \qquad\qquad 144.12 \div 6 \qquad\qquad 2\tfrac{1}{4} \div 3$$

    Correct Statements:

    a. _____

    b. _____

    c. _____

2. *Hurricane Tidbits*: Hurricanes are tropical cyclones with high velocity winds. Large amounts of water and high winds cause widespread destruction.

    a. Hurricanes are collectors. What do they collect? Unscramble the letters below to find out.

         mraw   sitom   ari

       They collect _____ _____ _____.

    b. Because hurricanes are collectors of (above answer), they certainly carry plenty of _ _ _ _ _ _ _ _ _ _ _ _ _ _.

ES–24
Ocean Speak

A. Complete each term related to the ocean by unscrambling the letters in the right column and writing them in the appropriate spaces next to the incomplete term in the left column. Also, write the letters—a, b, c, etc.—in the spaces at the left. Use the hints in parentheses to help you complete each term.

		Hint	Scrambled
____1.	submer_____	(research vessel)	a. ntlane
____2.	so_____	(sound pulses)	b. erni
____3.	ocean_____	(Robert Ballard)	c. toy
____4.	conti_____	(steep slope)	d. sys
____5.	subma_____	(deep canyon)	e. owt
____6.	tren_____	(Mariana)	f. -1C
____7.	ab_____	(ocean depths)	g. ragorhep
____8.	ma_____	(sea or oceans)	h. omt
____9.	sa_____	(salty)	i. nrie
____10.	gu_____	(flat seamount)	j. arn
____11.	cur_____	(moving water)	k. ntme
____12.	dia_____	(plant life)	l. npkalont
____13.	Na$^+$ and _____	(sea water ions)	m. lef
____14.	under_____	(irregular current)	n. blise
____15.	thermo_____	(temperature drop)	o. hc
____16.	sedi_____	(bottom matter)	p. sgbre
____17.	zoo_____	(eat phytoplankton)	q. pac
____18.	sh_____	(shallow sea)	r. nile
____19.	ice_____	(drifting ice)	s. licne
____20.	white_____	(white foam wave)	t. rnet

B. *Sea Animal Puzzlers:* Use the clues below to identify the sea organisms.

1. It's called a dollar yet can't be spent. _ _ _ _ _ _ _ _ _ _ _ (two words)

2. It's partly star but doesn't shine. _ _ _ _ _ _ _ _ (two words)

3. Has a "chin" but no face. _ _ _ _ _ _ _ _ _ _ (two words)

4. Carries a "ton" but weighs nearly zero. _ _ _ _ _ _ _ _ _ _

5. This animal's top is in the middle. _ _ _ _ _ _ _ _ _

ES–25
Sea Water

Saline means salty. Sea water is a saline liquid. If you accidentally gulp a mouthful of sea water, the taste may cause you to gag and cough. Let's take a closer look at the ingredients of sea water.

1. *Don't Drink the Water*: Salinity refers to the total salt content of the water. The main solid is sodium chloride, table salt. Other dissolved solids include magnesium chloride and calcium sulfate.

   Write the chemical symbols for the elements that combine to form each dissolved solid below. Place the symbols on each side of the + signs. You may need to refer to a Periodic table.

   ___ + ___   ___ + ___   ___ + ___
   magnesium chloride   calcium sulfate   sodium chloride

2. *How Much Salt?*: Sea water contains about 3.5 percent salts. Sea water salinity varies but the composition of sea water stays the same. What may cause a change in salinity? The conditions below may increase or decrease salinity. For each listed condition circle either INCREASES or DECREASES. Then give a reason for your choice on the line under the conditions.

Conditions	**Salinity**
sea water near hot area	a. INCREASES or DECREASES
_____	
rivers flow into sea	b. INCREASES or DECREASES
_____	
heavy evaporation	c. INCREASES or DECREASES
_____	
heavy precipitation	d. INCREASES or DECREASES
_____	
glaciers in sea water	e. INCREASES or DECREASES
_____	

3. *Salty Puzzler*: You evaporate 2,500 grams of sea water and receive 95 grams of dissolved salts. What was the salinity of the sea water? Salinity: _____ percent. Is this average sea water salinity? Circle one: YES   NO. Why or why not? _____
   _____

ES–26
Plankton in the Sea

Minute plankton are examples of drifters. These plant and animal organisms float in surface waters. They serve as a major food supply for many sea animals.

1. *Food for Thought*: Single-celled phytoplankton (minute plants) provide food for larger zooplankton (animal plankton). Fish of all sizes rely on plankton as the main source of nourishment. Use the clues to help you identify eight plankton-eating sea animals.

	Clues
P _ r _ _	bony surf fish
baleen _ _ _ **L** _	large mammal
_ l _ **A** _ _ _ e	tuna family
_ a _ _ _ **N** _	rhymes with cuisine
_ _ c **K** _ _ a _	pattern of wavy bands
T _ _ _	canned food
_ n _ _ **O** v _	eaten by sea birds
_ _ r _ _ **N** _	small silvery food fish

2. *So Big, So Small*: Imagine a 43-foot basking shark cruising near the surface hunting for plankton. The basking shark doesn't have "plankton vision" or secret radar for tracking these tiny organisms. So a question arises: How does it find and consume enough plankton to nourish its huge body? The statements in the box answer the question. Unfortunately, they are jumbled up and need to be placed in their correct order. Your job is to arrange the statements in their proper sequence. Use the spaces below to complete the task.

> plankton enters shark's stomach; water filtered through gills and strained for food; shark moving through water; plankton present in water; open mouth serves as a collecting unit; plankton dinner nourishes shark; shark swallows trapped plankton; plankton pass through mouth

a. _____

b. _____

c. _____

d. _____

e. _____

f. _____

g. _____

h. _____

ES–27
Sea Life: Pelagic Zone

The pelagic zone covers thousands of ocean miles. It extends just above the sea bottom to the surface. This area teems with life from microscopic sea organisms to mammals weighing several tons.

1. *Known Swimmers*:

   a. Six animals commonly found swimming in the pelagic zone are hidden in the puzzle. Lightly darken the letters spelling their names. Answers may be up, down, or backward. Use the I.D. Box to help you locate the names.

e	o	w	s	y
p	d	h	k	v
s	y	a	r	o
q	a	l	a	h
u	n	e	h	c
i	u	o	s	n
d	t	c	p	a

I.D. Box

whale	squid
krill	anchovy
tuna	copepods
plankton	rays
sardines	salmon
shark	dolfins

   b. The unshaded letters combine to spell the answer to this question:
   What animal plankton feeds on phytoplankton?

   Answer: _____. Here's a hint:

   You need not be smart like a fox,
   The answer's up there in the box.

2. *Seven Up*: The names of 15 pelagic animals appear below. Match seven of them to the clues. Write the name of the animal in the space to the left of the clues.

   Clues

   a. _____   rough skin, shark

   b. _____   tentacles, free swimmer

   c. _____   mammal, filter feeder

   d. _____   ink, tentacles, suckers

   e. _____   small tuna, food

   f. _____   sharp teeth, long

   g. _____   pinniped with flippers

squid	salmon	albacore	ray	eel
bass	whale	barracuda	swordfish	seal
jellyfish	dogfish	grouper	sculpin	turtle

(continued)

ES–27 (continued)

3. *Pelagic Puzzle*: The 15 letters show what happens to a herring when a hungry albacore appears. Describe what occurs.

a   h   l   e   b   r   a   r   c   i   o   n   r   g   e

_____

_____

_____

_____

_____

ES–28
Sea Life: Bottom Dwellers

Benthos refers to organisms that live on the sea floor. Clams, scallops, limpets, coral, and sea stars are examples of benthos organisms. Kelp, also known as seaweed, attaches itself to the sea floor. Large forests of kelp grow near the shore providing a "benthos bouquet" for many sea creatures.

1. *Six More on the Floor*: Circle six benthos organisms hidden in the letters below. They MUST be different from the examples given in the opening paragraph above.

   seahorseeelkelpabaloneseastarschitonplanktonreefbed
   coralseaanemonescallopswhitesharkoystersdiatonsmelt
   glamssnailspermwhaleblennymusselaureliasunfishperch

   HINT: The names rhyme with hustle, tale, Titan, cloister, key enemy, and matrimony.

2. *Benthos Banquet*: Bottom-dwelling organisms find food in different ways. Match the organism with the manner in which it gets food. Place the letter from the right column in the space to the left of the number. Some organisms use more than one method for acquiring food.

   Food-Getting Method

   _____ 1. sea anemone   a. eats rotting organisms

   _____ 2. crab   b. prefers to eat algae

   _____ 3. mussel   c. crushes shell, eats organism

   _____ 4. sea urchin   d. filters food from water

   _____ 5. barnacle   e. captures food with tentacles

   _____ 6. sponge   f. feeds on other animals

   _____ 7. sea star

3. *Benthos Puzzler*: There's a story of a boy whose first name is Neal. Interestingly, his last name is the same as the name of a common benthos organism. What is it? HINT: His first and last names come from the letters that spell the name of another common benthos animal: barnacle.

   His last name is __ __ __ __.   His full name is __ __ __ __   __ __ __ __.

ES–29
Sea Mammals, Part 1

A large variety of mammals live in the sea. Let's go on a mammal venture.

Marine Mammals: Complete the crossword puzzle, using information you know (or can find) about six different sea mammals.

ACROSS

2. Whales have a _____-blooded metabolism.
4. An area where seals breed.
5. Male seals and whales are called this.
8. The name for a whale's sonar system.
9. Large tropical mammal; eats seaweed.
10. Goes by the name "sea cow."

DOWN

1. The name given to baby whales.
3. Female seals and whales are called this.
5. Mouth structures in most whales.
6. Fur-bearing mammal; lives in ocean surf.
7. Intelligent mammal; beak-like snout.

Name _____   Date _____

ES–30
Sea Mammals, Part 2

Try your luck at solving the following three marine mammal puzzlers.

1. Darken the spaces in the box below where scrambled letters can be found that spell the answer to Question A. A letter may appear several times.

    Question A: What do you call the thick layer of fat under the skin of a whale?

    Answer: _____

t	r	e	b	v	b	u	r	o	r	e	l	c	u	e	r	o	b	k	u	d
n	d	u	w	g	r	s	m	h	u	d	l	t	j	l	s	j	l	o	e	f
g	p	r	z	d	u	b	t	c	u	e	i	m	h	e	p	f	u	e	l	s
s	f	b	k	w	b	a	q	z	r	p	j	i	m	l	o	k	e	t	r	w
y	x	l	v	h	l	e	e	a	e	b	r	d	t	u	g	p	r	a	b	c

    Question B: The darkened letters in the box above will answer this question: What does a sperm whale have that a baleen whale doesn't?
    Answer: A sperm whale has _____.

2. Darken the spaces in the box below to spell the answer to Question C. A letter may appear several times.

    Question C: A sea otter prefers two kinds of food. Abalone is one. What is the other choice meal?
    Answer: The other selection is sea _____.

i	h	c	k	n	i	u	e	c
l	h	u	i	p	r	t	u	e
n	s	h	n	t	c	r	s	r

    The unshaded letters combine to answer Questions D and E. The first four letters in Rows 1 and 2 (from top to bottom) answer Question D. The remaining five letters in Rows 2 and 3 answer Question E. Read the letters from left to right.

    Question D: What kind of beds do sea otters favor?
    Answer: They like _____ beds.

    Question E: What do you call the skeletons of the organisms in Question C?
    Answer: They are known as _____.

3. The seal and walrus belong to the Suborder Pinnipedia. A more commonly used term is _ _ _ _ _ _ _ _ _. Unscramble the circled letters in the statement below for the answer. HINT: The two terms are nearly identical.

    The elephant seal is the largest member of the group. The adult male displays his large nose during mating season.

Name _____   Date _____

ES–31
Tsunami

A tsunami, misnamed tidal wave, may occur when the sea shifts during an earthquake or when a volcano erupts. The sudden movements of the ocean floor agitate the surrounding water. The disturbed water begins to move rapidly. As energy builds, a wavelength of 60 or more miles from crest to crest forms. The stretched out wavelength or tsunami may travel 400 miles per hour or more in the open sea.

As the mass of speeding water nears the shore, it slows down and builds into a giant wall of water.

1. The stick man below is six feet tall. A 36-foot tsunami approaches him. Draw the height of the wave in relation to the height of the man.

2. What natural force may produce a 100- to 130-foot high tsunami? You can find the answer in the 26-letter puzzle below. CLUE: bottom right, top left.

e	k	a	u	q	n	u	s	e	h	t	m	o
r	f	t	e	n	a	l	p	d	r	i	h	t

3. A tsunami may destroy everything in its path. Use the letters in "tsunami" as the first letters to identify living organisms that may be injured or killed. The first one is done for you.

T   <u>trees, turtles, tarantulas</u>

S   _____

U   _____

N   _____

A   _____

M   _____

I   _____

36

ES–32
Physical Weathering

The breaking down and wearing away of rocks is known as weathering. Weathered rocks undergo physical and chemical changes. What processes create a physical change in rocks? What changes occur in rocks? The following activities will help you find out.

1. Weathering is a SLOW process. In time natural agents may break down a rock and cause it to crumble apart. Find the missing letters of the weathering agents below.

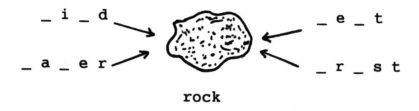

_ i _ d   _ e _ t

_ a _ e r   _ r _ s t

rock

2. Which of the following rocks show possible damage by physical weathering? Give a reason for your answer.

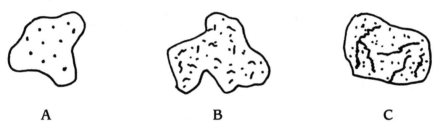

A   B   C

3. Plants may cause physical weathering to occur. The plant structure responsible for breaking rocks apart is hiding in the puzzle. Find and circle the answer.

s	t	a	m	e	n	v	e	i	n
a	n	t	h	e	r	l	e	a	f
c	o	t	b	l	o	s	s	o	m
b	a	t	v	i	o	l	e	t	e
n	o	p	i	s	t	i	l	o	m
s	e	e	d	f	r	u	i	t	a

4. Frost wedging occurs when water seeps into cracks in the rock. The water freezes and expands. Make a sketch to show what happens to the rock.

Name _____   Date _____

ES–33
Chemical Weathering

Chemical weathering occurs along with physical weathering. Chemical weathering takes place in the following manner:

1. **OXIDATION**—Iron particles in some rocks combine with oxygen to form rust, a yellowish brown material. As rust builds up, the rock weakens.

   Let a pencil point represent oxygen. The chemical symbol for iron is Fe. Use the pencil point to create "rust" on the rocks below. Simply shade the areas labeled Fe.

   a. What part of each rock will weather away first? Why?
   b. Why does rust cover only part of each rock?

2. **HYDRATION**—The chemical reaction of water with certain minerals in rocks. Rocks swell and crumble when hydration occurs.

   Rock A is in the beginning stages of hydration. Show what happens to the rock as hydration occurs by sketching the results in the boxes.

3. **CARBONATION**—Carbonic acid, a combination of carbon dioxide (CO_2) and water (H_2O), dissolves limestone or marble. A rock containing these minerals weakens and falls apart. How many carbon dioxide and water molecules can you make from the elements in the box?

H	O	O	C	H	C	C
C	O	H	O	C	H	C
O	H	C	H	O	O	O
C	O	H	H	C	H	O

   carbon dioxide molecules _____
   water molecules _____

4. *Brain Dissolver:* If you combined three carbon dioxide molecules with three water molecules from the elements in the box, how many of each element would be left?

ES–34
Getting into the Soil

The weathering process breaks down rocks into smaller particles. These fragments mix with decayed matter of once-living organisms. The combined materials further decompose to form a layer of soil at the surface of the earth.

1. *On Top*: The uppermost layer of soil is known as topsoil. Topsoil consists of weathered soil particles and humus, remains of once-living plants and animals. *Problem:* If it takes three centuries to form nine inches of topsoil, how many YEARS will it take to form 17 inches of topsoil?

   Answer: It will take about _____ years.

2. *Soil Toil*: Use the letters in ORGANIC to fill in the missing letters for each term in the chart. *Note:* Don't use the G, but it's okay to use the A twice.

Term	Description
b e d _ _ c k	solid, unweathered rock
m _ _ t l e r o c k	weathered rock above bedrock
_ l _ y	soil containing quartz particles
s _ l t	soil particles whose size lies between clay fragments and sand grains

3. *Pedalfer Puzzle*: Pedalfer soil contains aluminum and iron particles. Pedalfers occur in the middle latitudes. Create a way to show the presence of aluminum and iron in pedalfer soil.

4. *Slippery Question*: Ms. Daniels, science teacher, was describing to her third-period class how rock layers form. She asked, "Where would you find oil?" Marlene Dunes blurted out, "You'll always find oil in soil." Did Marlene give the correct answer? Why or why not?

ES–35
Three-Word Clue Erosion Puzzle

Rock material breaks and falls apart. The broken pieces are carried away and redeposited by natural forces. This process is known as erosion. Use the code below to decode each term related to erosion. To make it challenging, some of the letters have purposely been left out. The three-word clue will help you complete the puzzle.

> A = 1, B = 2, C = 3, D = 4, E = 5, F = 6, G = 7, H = 8,
> I = 9, J = 10, K = 11, L = 12, M = 13, N = 14, O = 15,
> P = 16, Q = 17, R = 18, S = 19, T = 20, U = 21, V = 22,
> W = 23, X = 24, Y = 25, Z = 26

Three-Word Clue

1. __ __ __ __ __ __   __ __ __ __ __
   18 14 9 7   1 5

Agent of erosion (2 words)

2. __ __ __ __   __ __ __ __ __ __
   19   12   18 19   14

Overgrazing causes this (2 words)

3. __ __ __ __ __ __ __
   20   19 15

Loose, porous soil

4. __ __ __ __   __ __ __ __ __
   4   19   20 15

Destruction by wind (2 words)

5. __ __ __ __ __ __ __
   18   9 20

Agent of erosion

6. __ __ __ __ __ __ __ __ __
   16 14   12 1   14

Old eroded mountain

7. high __ __ __ __ __ __ __
           16 1   1 21

Subject to erosion

8. __ __ __ __ __ __
   18 14 6

Water, excessive amount

9. __ __ __ __ __ __ __   __ __ __
   12 1   12   5

Agent of erosion (2 words)

10. __ __ __ __ __
    18 5 16

Slow soil movement

11. __ __ __ __
    5 1

Eroded plateau product

12. __ __ __ __
    9 4

Agent of erosion

Name _____   Date _____

ES–36
Fun with Water

The colorless, transparent liquid known as water provides a creative challenge to those who enjoy solving problems. Try your hand at finding the answers to the following problems.

1. *Go Figure*: Give a title for each sketch.

    A.   **B.**   **C.**

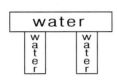   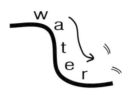   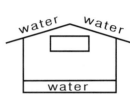

_____ _____   _____   _____

2. *Fill the Void*: Complete the statement with four of these eight words: carbon, oxygen, mixture, compound, hydrogen, liquid, chemically, nitrogen.

_____ and _____ combine _____

to form the _____ water.

3. *Get a Clue*: Use the clues to complete the words related in some way to water.

                                                           Clues

    w _ _ _   hole below water table

    _ **a** _ _ _ _   swift moving liquid

    _ **t** _ _ _   100 degrees C or 212 degrees F

    _ _ **e**   0 degrees C or 32 degrees F

    _ _ **r** _ _ _   natural flow of groundwater

4. *Limited Liquid*:

    a. How many molecules of water can be produced from the letters in the following message?

        HENRY, ROXANNE, ANDY, AND THELMA ORDERED ANCHOVY PIZZA. HOORAY!

        _____ molecules of water

    b. How many molecules of water can be produced from these letters?

        H y e g y O h g H o x n H O n e H o r d H

        _____ molecules of water

ES–37
Ice Age

An ice age is a period of extreme cold. Sheets of ice covered large areas of land. Ice sheets have advanced and retreated several times in recent geologic history. This occurred because the climate switched from cold to warm and back again. The last ice age ended about 11,000 years ago. Glaciers, of course, thrive under ice-age conditions.

1. *Cool Words*: Circle six of the 19 following words that relate in some way to the formation of an ice age. Use your creative-thinking ability for two of the words.

expense	chlorine	mercury	time	water
oxygen	tsunami	root	upheaval	lichen
sandstone	freeze	salt	alloy	metal
granite	temperature	hydrogen	melt	

2. *Turnabout*: Why do you think an ice sheet might slow down or stop, then retreat? Use the letters scattered around the ice sheet to complete the statement below.

A w_ _ _ _ _ _ _   c_ _ _ _ _ _ _ could cause an ice sheet to act this way.

3. *What's to Blame?*: Scientists believe ice ages may be caused by small, regular changes in Earth's orbit and in the tilt of the Earth's axis. They say these changes produce a cooling effect. During the last ice age, ice and snow covered more than three-tenths of the world's land surface. The figure below represents the Earth's land mass. Darken the approximate amount of ice and snow coverage on the figure.

4. *Frosty Riddle:* What do glaciers use to stay cold at night?

ES–38
Glaciers

1. A glacier is a huge mass of ice and snow found in cold areas. A natural force causes the glacier to do something. Lightly darken the letters in the box that spell the name of the force. The unshaded letters will reveal what the force causes the glacier to do. Place answers in the spaces below the box.

f	g	r	l	a	o	v	i	t	w	y

_ _ _ _ _ _ _ causes a glacier to _ _ _ _.

2. The stress on a moving glacier causes the surface ice to break. When this happens, deep cracks form. These are known as _ _ _ _ _ _ _ _ _ _. Use the letters in CRESS and SAVE to fill in the spaces.

3. Glaciers found in mountain areas are called alpine glaciers. As they move through valleys between mountains, they carve and gouge out hunks of crustal material. In eight words or less, describe HOW an alpine glacier can change a V-shaped valley into a U-shape. You MUST use these words in your description: weight, massive, size.

4. Glaciers _ _ _ _ _ land as they move over it. Unscramble the following "sign" to recover the letters necessary to spell out the answer.

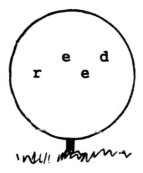

5. *Brain Bogler:* If a glacier moves 3,000 feet in eight years, about how many miles will it travel in 50 years? (5,280 feet = one mile)

_____ miles

43

ES–39
Minerals

Five letters spell CRUST, the solid, rocky shell of the Earth. Minerals occur naturally in the Earth's crust.

1. Use the clues to identify the minerals below. Each mineral name needs two or more letters from the word CRUST. Fill in the blanks with the missing letters.

Mineral

a. _ _ l f _ Ⓔ
b. g _ a p h i _ e
c. _ _ _ i l e
d. b a _ x i _ e
e. _ e _ p e Ⓝ _ i n e
f. b a _ i _ e
g. Ⓜ _ _ _ o v i _ e
h. _ _ p _ i _ e
i. a z _ _ Ⓘ _ e
j. f l _ o _ i _ Ⓔ
k. _ h o d o n Ⓘ _ e
l. o _ _ h o c l a _ e
m. c a _ _ i _ e _ i _ e
n. _ _ _ q _ Ⓞ i _ e
o. _ o _ _ Ⓝ d _ m
p. _ o _ _ m a l i n e
q. _ h e _ _

Clues

1. yellow; found in matches
2. pure carbon; pencil lead
3. TiO_2; titanium ore
4. aluminum ore; fairly soft
5. yellow or green; used as decorative stone
6. $BaSO_4$: "heavy spar"
7. mica; elastic, flexible
8. red copper ore
9. bluish copper ore
10. number 4 on hardness scale
11. shades of pink; prized as ornamental stones
12. feldspar; used in pottery and glass industries
13. SnO_2; tin ore
14. greenish blue; semi-precious stone
15. ruby and sapphire
16. used in gemstones and optical equipment
17. variety of quartz; known as hornstone

2. *Brain Buzzer:* If CRUST lost its C, it would become RUST. What mineral combined with oxygen forms RUST? Use FOUR of the eight circled letters to show your answer.

— — — —

3. *Double Brain Buzzer:* Use the remaining four letters to identify a large excavation made in the earth to remove minerals.

— — — —

Name _____   Date _____

ES–40
Gemstones

The mineral world prides itself by producing rare, beautiful crystals for all to enjoy. Many of these prized jewels find a home in rings, bracelets, and necklaces.

1. *Shining Examples*: A gem of high quality captures the attention of many people. Unquestionably, a desirable gem becomes precious and valuable. Identify eight different "precious" gems. Use the clues to help you find the answers.

	Clues
_ **P** _ _	fiery play of colors
_ _ _ **R** _	products of clams and oysters
_ _ **E** _ _ _ _	deep green; beryl variety
C _ _ _ _ _ _	yellow crystals; false topaz
_ **I** _ _ _ _ _	hardest substance; pure carbon
_ **O** _ _ _	hardness of 8; various colors
_ **U** _ _	deep red; corundum
S _ _ _ _ _ _ _	blue; corundum

2. *A Ten!*: As a gem becomes popular, its value increases. Other factors determine the value of a gem. Unscramble the words in parentheses below to reveal what they are.

    the _____ (ezsi), lack of _____ (wfsal), beauty of _____ (cloro) and _____ (erlstu), _____ (snahersd), and perfection of _____ (cylastr) shape

3. *Gem Dandy*: Use the letters scattered in all three rocks below to produce five gems. (Be careful: A trick lies ahead.)

    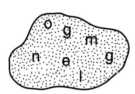 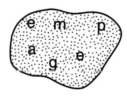 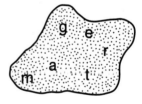

    The gems strewn about in the rocks are _____, _____, _____, _____, and _____.

4. *Bonus Puzzler*: Opal Casey, gemologist, cut a 10-carat diamond into four sections. Surprisingly, she admitted that she could get only ONE gem from a gemstone. How could this be?

ES–41

Rock Talk

If you ask someone, "What is a rock?" you may hear: "A hard stonelike thing" or "A piece of earth." A geologist might answer, "A single mineral or mixture of minerals." Simply, a rock is a solid substance made up of minerals.

What are minerals? Minerals are various materials formed in nature and have definite patterns. Examples are quartz, calcite, and gypsum.

1. *Mineral Mix*: Each diagram shows a combination of minerals. Which diagram—A, B, or C—does the best job of producing a ROCK? Give a reason for your answer. HINT: Put your problem-solving skills to work!

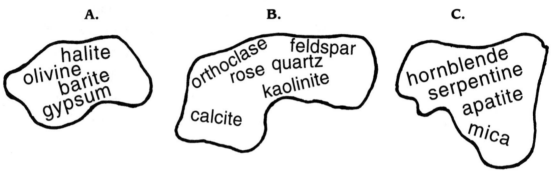

2. *Where's the DNA?*: Some rocks are easier to identify than others. Which diagram— A, B, or C—offers the easiest rock to identify? Give a reason for your answer.

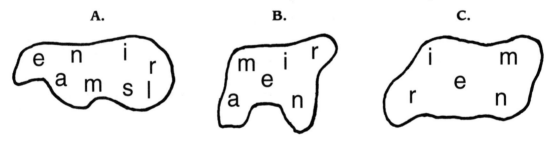

3. *Stack 'Em Up*: Many rocks contain quartz, a common mineral. Sandstone, a sedimentary rock, turns into quartzite under heat and pressure. Which diagram— A, B, or C—represents the best producer of rocks? Give a reason for your answer.

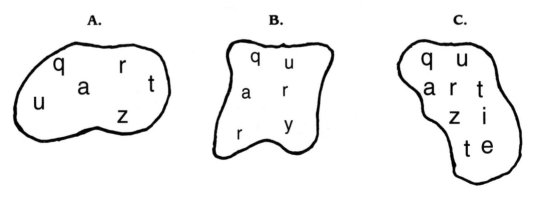

© 2001 by The Center for Applied Research in Education

ES–42
Igneous Intrusion

Hot molten magma from the Earth's crust reaches the surface through volcanic eruptions. Magma cools and hardens into igneous rock. INTRUSIVE igneous rock cools deep below the crust. The slow cooling produces coarse-grained rock with large crystals. EXTRUSIVE igneous rock cools quickly on the Earth's surface. Fast cooling produces fine-grained rock with small crystals or no crystals at all. Many igneous rocks contain a mixture of small and large mineral grains.

1. *Grain Strain:* Fill in Figures A and B with a combination of mineral grains and crystals. Use the description above to help you.

   A. Instrusive Igneous Rock   **B.** Extrusive Igneous Rock

2. *Touch and Such:* Texture refers to how a rock looks and feels. Texture depends on the size, shape, and position of mineral grains in a rock. Write INTRUSIVE or EXTRUSIVE for each of the following texture descriptions.

   a. _____ large, broken crystals; coarse grains

   b. _____ glassy, smooth

   c. _____ porous, rough, lightweight

   d. _____ tiny crystals, heavy; fine grains

3. *Down and Up:* Granite is the most common intrusive igneous rock. The most abundant extrusive igneous rock is basalt. What minerals may be found in these rocks? Use the clues to reveal the minerals. Place the number of the mineral in each diagram below.

Clues

GRANITE: four-lettered mineral; equals 2 pints+z; unscramble: caheorsotl

BASALT: letters 2, 3, and 4 mean "linger"; rhymes with scene; sounds like "rocks" in the middle

Minerals

1. mica
2. olivine
3. orthoclase feldspar
4. plagioclase feldspar
5. pyroxine
6. quartz

Granite

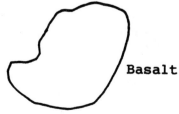

Basalt

ES–43
Mighty Metamorphic

Metamorphic rocks form when preexisting rocks undergo heat, pressure, and chemical action in the Earth's crust. For example, heat and pressure can change limestone, a sedimentary rock, into marble, a metamorphic rock. Under similar conditions, shale, a sedimentary rock, may become slate, a metamorphic rock. This process is known as metamorphism.

1. *Metamorphic Mania:* Use the clues to complete the puzzle.

ACROSS:
2. turns into slate
3. turns into marble
4. common igneous rock
5. splits or cleaves into layers

DOWN:
1. this rock becomes quartzite
4. a coarse rock with bands and streaks

2. *Fossil Squish:* Fossils may be found in limestone and sandstone. Rock containing fossils are called fossiliferous. If a fossiliferous rock experiences metamorphic change, the fossils may be torn, twisted, and stretched beyond recognition.

    This figure shows an imprint of a fossil fish in rock. Use the box to the right to sketch how the fish might change during metamorphism.

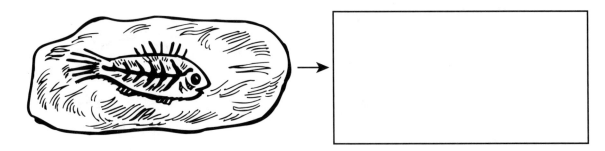

Name _____   Date _____

ES–44
Sedimentary Inquiry

Natural events like wind and rain break down rock into small fragments called sediments. In time, these particles compress and stick together. The sediment flattens into layers known as strata. As sediment piles up, the layers press together to form sedimentary rock. Some sediments result from chemical reactions at the Earth's surface.

1. *What's Next?*: Use the information in the paragraph above to help you put these phrases describing the formation of sedimentary rock in their correct order. Place the letter opposite the first step in Space 1, the letter next to the second step in Space 2, and so forth.

a. layers of sediment form	e. sedimentary rock develops
b. rock fragments cement together	f. rock fragments compress
c. rock fragments build up	g. rock fragments present
d. rock fragments carried in moving water	h. increased pressure due to gravity

Sedimentary rock may form in the following manner:

1. _____   2. _____   3. _____   4. _____   5. _____   6. _____   7. _____   8. _____

2. *Stagnant Fragment:* The names of seven sedimentary rocks are broken and scattered about. Use the clues to help you put the names back together.

Clues	Sedimentary Rock
1. collection of pebbles	a. _____
2. gritty, fine-grained	b _____
3. made of calcite and shells	c. _____
4. calcium carbonate	d. _____
5. flaky, clay-sized particles	e. _____
6. plant remains	f. ____
7. cemented sand grains	g. _____

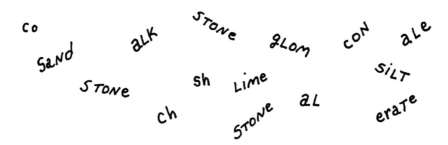

ES–45
Diastrophism

1. Movement of the solid parts of the earth is known as diastrophism. When certain areas of land lift or rise several feet, we call this **UPLIFTING.**

    Connect 12 or more dots in the box to show an example of UPLIFTING.

    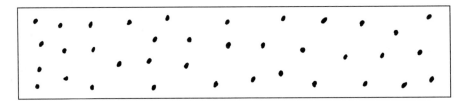

    a.   What earth forces may cause uplifting to occur?

    b.   Name two earth features created by rising land.

2. **SUBSIDENCE** or sinking of land occurs when the earth's crust sinks or drops several feet.

    Connect 12 or more dots in the box to show an example of SUBSIDENCE.

    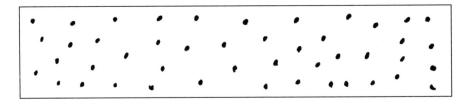

    a.   What earth forces may cause land to sink or drop?

    b.   Name two earth features caused by sinking land.

3. **THRUST** happens when large masses of rock move past each other in a horizontal direction. The movement produces shock waves that spread out in all directions. The waves are known as earthquakes.

    Darken TWO areas in the box and use TWO arrows to show an example of THRUST.

    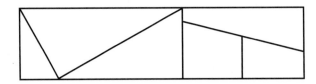

    What earth forces may cause thrust movement?

Name _____ Date _____

ES-46
Mountains and Hills

1. *Maybe a Mountain, Perhaps a Hill*: Write the letters of the statements describing mountains in the space to the right of the word MOUNTAINS. Write the letters of the statements describing hills in the space to the right of the word HILLS. Some statements apply to both mountains and hills.

   MOUNTAINS: _____

   HILLS: _____

   ---

   a. May result from uplifting action.
   b. May be eroded by water over time.
   c. A natural raised part of the earth.
   d. Features massive and rugged structures.
   e. Usually less than 2,000 feet in elevation.
   f. The tops are more rounded than jagged.
   g. These are known to form ranges.
   h. May feature many peaks and valleys.
   i. Small mounds of sediment.
   j. Usually 2,000 feet or higher in elevation.
   k. May result from volcanic activity.
   l. May result from folding action.
   m. May be the result of faulting.
   n. May influence weather conditions.
   o. May result from plate collision.
   p. A well-known earth landform.
   q. May show evidence of combined earth forces.

   ---

   a. Use three or four statements for MOUNTAINS to define mountains. Mountains are

   _____

   _____

   b. Use three or four statements for HILLS to define hills. Hill are

   _____

   _____

2. *Graph It:* Use the information from MOUNTAINS and HILLS to complete profiles for a mountain and a hill on the graphs below.

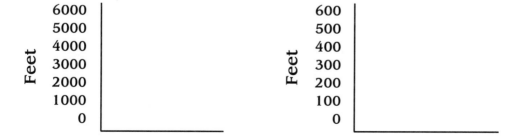

51

ES–47
Moving Continents

In 1912, a scientist named Alfred Wegener proposed a theory about how continents drifted apart and moved to where they are today. This idea became known as the Continental Drift Theory. Wegener believed all the continents were joined together in a single landmass. He called the landmass Pangaea.

1. For Part 1, list two examples of EARTH FEATURES for each of the 13 letters. Use the letters to serve as beginning letters for each feature. The first one is done for you. Use the same procedure for Part 2, except this time list two examples of MINERALS found in the earth's crust.

Part 1		Part 2	
A	alluvial fan, atoll	P	_____
L	_____	A	_____
F	_____	N	_____
R	_____	G	_____
E	_____	A	_____
D	_____	E	_____
		A	_____
W	_____		
E	_____		
G	_____		
E	_____		
N	_____		
E	_____		
R	_____		

2. *Brain Drifter:* Rocky Stone, miner, found a green mineral he called "phosphate," number five on the scale of hardness. Rocky lost his mineral a short time later. The loss troubled him deeply. In fact, he couldn't eat for the next three days. Why did Rocky have a tough time eating? HINT: Look to the name of the mineral.

3. The ideas of continental drift are described in a more recent theory known as

    _ _ _ _ _ _ _ _ _ _ _ _ _ _ _.

    The answer is hidden in the following series of letters:

    platedriftseafloortectonicsridgeseparatedcrust

© 2001 by The Center for Applied Research in Education

ES–48
Landforms

A landform is a surface feature on the earth's crust. It makes up the shape of the land. Natural forces produce landforms.

1. *Begin with the Basics*: A plateau is a high, fairly flat area next to a mountain. It represents a basic landform. Two more examples of basic landforms are hidden in the 15 letters below. What are they? HINT: One is hiding inside the other.

m o p l u n a i t a n s i n s

The two landforms are _____ and _____.

2. *Forces at Work*: Nature's forces continually change the shape of the land. List the forces responsible for the changes shown in the following diagrams. Use the space under each sketch to write your answer.

a.

Forces: _____

b.

Forces: _____

c.

Forces: _____

d.

Forces: _____

3. *Landform Puzzler*: You can create two landforms from these eight letters: bchyleav. What two? HINT: Rhymes with "Sally Peach." You may use a letter more than once.

ES–49
Volcanic Magic

Molten rock known as magma comes to the surface and spreads over land and water. Magma becomes lava once it flows out on the surface of the Earth.

1. *Mysterious Magma*:

   a. Put these words in their proper order to describe magma: liquid, mass, rock, hot.

      Magma may be described as a _____ _____ _____ _____.

   b. Ms. Garcia, science teacher, asked Dan the following question: "What may cause a large mass of rock to melt?" Dan replied, "The atmosphere?" Sorry, Dan. Wrong answer. However, all is not lost. The correct response is hidden in Dan's answer. Find and circle it.

2. *Very Volcanic*: A volcano is an opening in the Earth's crust through which an eruption occurs. Circle the eight words scattered within the volcanic cone that relate to volcanic eruptions.

3. *Build a Cone*: The three main types of volcanic cones are described in Column A. Column B contains the pieces needed to put each type together. Use the pieces from Column B to create a sketch of each type of volcanic cone. Place drawings in Column C.

Type	A	B	C
Shield	gentle at slopes broad at base dome shape		Shield
Cinder	steep sides narrow base cone shape		Cinder
Composite	shape somewhere between shield cone and cinder cone		Composite

4. *Red Hot Riddle:* What do you call an extinct volcano?

ES–50
Volcanic Attack

Volcanoes are powerful reminders that Earth remains geologically active. An erupting volcano may destroy any living organisms for miles around.

PROBLEM: Volcano Insano blew its top. The force of the eruption did something strange: It caused all of the vowels for the words related to volcanoes listed below to disappear. Replace the vowels and restore each word to its original form. Use the descriptions on the right to help you complete the task.

Volcanic Words	Descriptions
1. t _ p h r _	ejected volcanic material
2. _ b s _ d _ _ n	volcanic glass
3. f _ s s _ r _	lava flows through this
4. p _ m _ c _	porous volcanic rock
5. m _ g m _	molten rock
6. w _ t _ r v _ p _ r	volcanic gas
7. c _ n d _ r s	coarse volcanic fragments
8. c r _ t _ r	depression, top of volcano
9. b _ s _ l t	lava rock
10. c _ r b _ n d _ _ x _ d _	volcanic gas
11. c _ n _	volcanic structure
12. _ x p l _ s _ v _	violent eruption
13. _ _ z _ n g	quiet eruption
14. _ c t _ v _	recent eruption
15. d _ r m _ n t	sleeping volcano
16. _ x t _ n c t	nonactive volcano
17. c _ m p _ s _ t _	lava and cinder cones
18. c _ l d _ r _	basinlike depression
19. s c _ r _ _	porous, cinderlike lava
20. s h _ _ l d	broad-based volcano

Shade the letters in the box that spell the names of two volcanoes: VESUVIUS (Italy) and SURTSEY (Iceland). Unscramble the unshaded letters to spell the answer to the mystery question.

S	T	U	Y	I	S	E
O	R	S	V	R	U	T
E	S	V	T	U	S	A

Mystery Question: What is the name given to a volcano formed by flows of lava, ash, cinders, and rock fragments?

Answer: It is a _ _ _ _ _ _ -volcano.

ES–51
Earthquake Lingo

The strain on crustal rocks may cause them to break and move apart. The vibrations created by this movement are called earthquakes.

Use the letters in EARTHQUAKE DAMAGE to help you identify terms related to earthquakes. The clues will assist you in filling in the blanks with the correct answers.

Clues

_ _ _ _ _ E _   Scale measuring magnitude

S   _ A _ _   Slow-moving seismic action

_ _ R _ _ _   Causes rocks to break

_ _ _ _ T   Movement along break in rock

_ _ _ _ _ _ H _ _ _   After earthquake tremors

Q _ _ _ _   Ground tremble

_ _ _ U _   Slippage along a fault

_ _ A _ _ _ _ _   The breaking of rocks

K _ _ _ _ _ _   Energy of motion

_ _ E _ _ _   A shaking action

_ _ _   _ _ D _ _ _ _   California fault (2 words)

P   _ A _ _   Fast-moving seismic wave

_ _ _ _ M _ _   Means shake or shock

_ A _ _ _ _ _ _ _   Measure of earthquake energy

_ _ _ _ G _   Force behind earthquakes

_ _ _ _ E _ _ _ _   Point directly above earthquake

© 2001 by The Center for Applied Research in Education

Earthquake Riddles

1. What did one earthquake say to another?

2. If you don't live in earthquake country, what kind of insurance do you need?

ES–52
Fossils

1. A fossil is the preserved remains of a once-living organism from a past geologic period. What CAN and CANNOT become a fossil? Unscramble the ten 4-letter words and write them on the lines. Place a *PF* for *Probable Fossil* and *NW* for *No Way* in the parentheses to the right of each word.

   a. ogrf _____ ( )   f. lacy _____ ( )

   b. esde _____ ( )   g. snik _____ ( )

   c. ocrk _____ ( )   h. ribd _____ ( )

   d. olis _____ ( )   i. roni _____ ( )

   e. fren _____ ( )   j. sihf _____ ( )

2. Soft insect parts have been preserved in amber, the hardened resin of ancient trees. Complete the names of four insect parts found in amber.

   _ _ d _ _ e _   _ n _ _ _ _ _ a _

   (2 words) _ a _ _ i _ _   _ e _ _   _ h _ _ a _

3. ALL of the following organisms have been found as fossils. CIRCLE the plants and UNDERLINE the animals.

horsetail	sea lily	mollusk
diatoms	pecten	lepidodendron

4. What would ONE of these girls have to do to become the preserved remains of an ancient organism?

   Marge   Flossi   Leona   Carla   Sasha   Kristin

5. Rona Suid told her friend, Jenna, that she could easily become a dinosaur. Rona said she could prove it with a pencil and paper. What do you think Rona did?

6. A scientist found 12 dinosaur footprints. She measured ONLY one of them. How long was it?

7. Create an animal fossil from the letters in these words: nail, foil, mass. You must use every letter in all three words. HINT: The answer has two 6-lettered words.

8. *Paleontology Puzzler:* What is the hardest part of a fossilized crossopterygian fish?

ES–53
Prehistoric Organisms

All of the plants and animals listed below lived during ancient times. Match the organisms in the left column with the paired rhyme descriptions in the right column. Place the number of the description on the line.

Organisms	Paired Rhyme Descriptions
_____ a. sponge	1. hairy beast; now deceased
_____ b. petrified wood	2. three horns on top; thanks, mom and pop
_____ c. woolly mammoth	3. scorpion me; Silurian Sea
_____ d. Triceratops	4. a squirrel's home; turned to stone
_____ e. eurypterid	5. full of pores; lived near shores
_____ f. starfish	6. cedar or pine; a plant divine
_____ g. sequoia	7. a sea lily; seems quite silly
_____ h. trilobite	8. a "second brain"; cerebral fame
_____ i. gastropod	9. palmlike, indeed; came from a seed
_____ j. crinoid	10. marine lizard; aqueous wizard
_____ k. conifer	11. three-lobed distinct; now most extinct
_____ l. Mosasaur	12. a spiral shell; houses me well
_____ m. Stegosaurus	13. a netlike structure; so easy to rupture
_____ n. cycad	14. no flim-flam here; it's a clam, my dear
_____ o. forams	15. while geologists toil; we point to oil
_____ p. bryozoan	16. a ducklike bill; has swimming skill
_____ q. Hadrosaur	17. a Pacific Coast hood; cozy home to redwood
_____ r. pelecypod	18. many tube feet; not too discreet

Brain Pain: What would you get if you crossed a crinoid (sea lily) with an ancient parasite?

ES–54

Precambrian Era
Geologic Time Scale, Part 1
4.5 billion–600 million years ago

An era is the largest unit of geological time. Eras are subdivided into periods. Periods are divided into epochs.

1. *Timely Puzzle*: How does the advertisement "Choose Pride Pears" relate to geologic time? CLUE: Reread the first paragraph.

2. *Very, Very, Very Old Rocks*: Precambrian rocks exist in many areas around the world. Most of these large rock shields have undergone folding and faulting, the results of extensive metamorphism.

   The figure represents a 50-mile mass of rock. Use the box to the right to show how metamorphism might change the appearance of the rock mass.

3. *Precambrian Thought-Provoker*: Read the following statements regarding life in the Precambrian Era:

   • At best, the fossil record is poor.
   • Soft-bodied organisms such as worms and jellyfish may have existed during this time.
   • The fossils of algae-like organisms have been found in Precambrian rock.
   • Shield rocks contain graphite, a carbon mineral. Plants and animals are a source of carbon.

   Use clues from the above statements to complete each term in the puzzle.
   The completed terms offer evidence to support the possible existence of life in the Precambrian Era.

$$\_\ \ l\ \_\ \_\ \_$$
$$\_\ \_\ \_\ \_\ \_\ \ i\ \_\ \_$$
$$f\ \_\ \_\ \_\ \_\ \_\ \_$$
$$\_\ \ e\ \_\ \_\ \_\ \_\ \_\ \_\ \_$$

4. *Look Within:* What does this group of letters show?

   P r l e c i a m f b r e i a n

ES–55
Paleozoic Era
Geologic Time Scale, Part 2
600 million years–270 million years ago

The Paleozoic Era is divided into seven periods. Each period is marked by the rising and sinking of land. New forms of plant and animal life appeared over 330 million years.

1. *Paleozoic Puzzle*: The following statements describe a condition or organism that existed during the Paleozoic Era. The answers appear in the puzzle. Write each answer in the space to the right of the statement. Then darken the answer in the puzzle. Answers may be up, down, backward, or forward.

   a. The sea organism known to build a solid ridge at or near the surface of the water. _ _ _ _ _

   b. A solid ridge of stony skeletons secreted by certain marine organisms. _ _ _ _ _

   c. The temperature of some Paleozoic seas. _ _ _ _

   d. The ability to adjust to an environment. _ _ _ _ _ _

   e. A creature of great size and strength. _ _ _ _ _ _

   f. A scaly organism with fins and gills. _ _ _ _ _

   g. A slow-moving, spiral-shelled organism. _ _ _ _ _ _

   h. A name for some bivalve mollusks. _ _ _ _ _ _

   i. Known as seaweed and pond scum. _ _ _ _ _ _

   j. A large cartilaginous fish with tough skin. _ _ _ _ _ _

s	h	a	r	k	s	c	l	a	m	s	v	a	d	a	p	t
	f	e	r	n	w	o	s	k	s	u	l	l	o	m	f	
	f	i	s	h	a	r	e	e	f	t	i	g	i	a	n	t
t	o	o	r		m	a	o	h	s	a	f	a	w	k	c	
w	a	r	m		p	l	i	a	n	s	e	e	a	b	s	

   The darkened boxes describe a large body of salt water known as a

   _____.

2. *Come Out, Come Out*: Find the Paleozoic sea critters hiding in the seaweed forest. CLUE: What's another name for seaweed?

   a. a s l p o g n a g e e   _ _ _ _ _ _

   b. a m o l l g l u a s k e   _ _ _ _ _ _ _ _

   c. a f l i g s a h e   _ _ _ _ _

   d. a j e l l l g y f a i s h e _ _ _ _ _ _ _ _ _ _

© 2001 by The Center for Applied Research in Education

ES–56

Mesozoic Era

Geologic Time Scale, Part 3
(230–180 million years ago)

The Mesozoic Era, known as the Age of Reptiles, includes three periods of geologic history: Triassic, Jurassic, and Cretaceous.

1. *Classic Triassic:* A widespread development of plants and animals occurred during the Triassic Period. The following organisms lived during this period:

   ANIMALS: dinosaurs, birds, mammals, protozoans, sponges, gastropods, pelecypods, arthropods, ammonites, crinoids, and echinoids

   PLANTS: cycads, conifers, ferns, and scouring rushes

   Select seven organisms to represent the Triassic Period. Which seven? A clue lies in this "Mesozoic Message."

   > Before you decide to "toss in the towel,"
   > Look once more to the second-letter vowel.

   The seven organisms are _____, _____,
   _____, _____, _____,
   _____, and _____.

2. *Jurassic Jumbos:* Dinosaurs ruled during the Jurassic Period. Fossil evidence shows the existence of two major dinosaur groups. What did they eat? Some ate _____; other preferred _____. Unscramble the numbers and letters for the answers.

   $$l + m + n + 2\ t's + e + p + 2\ a's + s$$

3. *Cretaceous Exit:* Many organisms, including the dinosaurs, became extinct at the end of the Mesozoic Era. Extinction may have been caused by widespread (sca cids) _____, (clam citi) _____ change, the rise of (mam slam) _____, or meteorite (cam pit) _____.

   Unscramble the letters in parentheses to spell the one-word answers. Place the answers on the lines.

4. *Mesozoic Riddle:* What remains at the end of Cretaceous?

ES–57

Cenozoic Era

Geologic Time Scale, Part 4
(65 million years ago–present)

The Cenozoic Era is known as the Age of Mammals. Crustal activity, climate changes, and mammals evolved during this time.

1. *No More Than Four*: The names of four plants, four invertebrates (animals without backbones), and four vertebrates (animals with backbones) are separated into four columns. Assemble the names and write them in ALPHABETICAL ORDER in the blanks.

mus	tiles	rep	phib
gras	sects	ders	spi
le	cy	murs	in
pa	star	se	fish
press	lms	moths	ses
mam	ians	am	sels
quoias			

PLANTS: _ _ _ _ _ _ _ _, _ _ _ _ _ _ _ _ _, _ _ _ _ _ _, and

_ _ _ _ _ _ _ _

INVERTEBRATES: _ _ _ _ _ _ _ _, _ _ _ _ _ _ _ _,

_ _ _ _ _ _ _ _, and _ _ _ _ _ _ _ _ _

VERTEBRATES: _ _ _ _ _ _ _ _ _ _ _ _, _ _ _ _ _ _ _,

_ _ _ _ _ _ _ _ _, and _ _ _ _ _ _ _ _ _

2. *Pleistocene Frostbite*: The climate turned very cold about two million years ago. Ice sheets covered nearly one-fourth of all land. Fossil remains of two mystery animals have been found buried in huge blocks of ice. Who are these mysterious creatures? Hints appear "frozen" in the glacier below. Use the clues to help you identify the names of the animals. Write their names in the empty spaces.

One of the Cenozoic beasts is a _ _ _ _ _ _ _ _ _ _ _ _ _ _.

The other is known as a _ _ _ _ _ _ _ _ _.

3. *Cenozoic Riddle:* What part of a Cenozoic elephant has no bones?

Part II

Life Science

LS–1
Life

A living organism—plant or animal—has special properties or features that distinguish it from nonliving matter. The puzzle answers will reveal some of these characteristics.

1. *Six Down, One Across*

   ACROSS:

   7. The food-making process of plants

   DOWN:

   1. Organisms do this to their environment
   2. An organism's reaction to a stimulus
   3. This produces a reaction in an organism
   4. The power source of an organism
   5. To make an organism stronger or more effective
   6. The period of time an organism lives (two words)

2. *More than One*: Organisms are cells, cells, cells, cells, and more cells. This statement can be summed up in a 13-letter word: lmueitlecelllariu. Oops! There are four extra letters. So we need to get rid of them. But which ones? Use the following message to help you remove the extra letters:

   Cross out letter "e," number one; then wipe away "le" just for fun.
   Letter "i" before the "u" (needs to go) . . . now you're through.

   Rearrange the letters to spell __ __ __ __ __ __ __ __ __ __ __ __ __.

3. *It's Alive!*: Circle the living organisms hidden in the following terms:

a.	appearance	j.	cashew
b.	triumphant	k.	signature
c.	clasp	l.	dynamite
d.	trampoline	m.	street
e.	femur	n.	configure
f.	share	o.	supine
g.	clamp	p.	scooter
h.	ticket	q.	blouse
i.	scratcher	r.	confiscate

LS–2
Cells, Part 1

A cell is the smallest unit of an organism capable of carrying on certain life functions.

1. *One, Two, Three . . .*

   a. Underline four members of the following group known to exist as single cells.

      worm   sponge   vacuole   bacterium   blood   petiole
      paramecium   mitochondria   nerve   fern   flagellum

   b. Underline four members of the following group recognized as many-celled organisms.

      amoeba   virus   jellyfish   tapeworm   protist   ant
      euglena   mosquito   rotifer   volvox   moneran   proton

2. *Connect 'Em*: Match the cell structure in the left column with its function in the right column. Place the matching letter in the space next to the cell structure.

Cell Structure	Function
_____1. cell membrane	a. Involved in enzyme activity
_____2. cytoplasm	b. Stores food and water
_____3. mitochondria	c. Directs cellular activity
_____4. nucleus	d. Contains structures that carry out life processes
_____5. vacuole	e. Protection and support

3. *Cell Stuff*: Unscramble the single or paired words in parentheses to produce a term to match the description.

   a. (Miss Soo) Diffusion of water through a membrane: _ _ _ _ _ _ _

   b. (is moist) Cellular division: _ _ _ _ _ _ _ _

   c. (suites) Group of cells: _ _ _ _ _ _ _

   d. (berm name) Cell lining: _ _ _ _ _ _ _ _ _

   e. (sun clue) Control center of cell: _ _ _ _ _ _ _ _

   f. (client roe) Involved in animal cell reproduction: _ _ _ _ _ _ _ _ _ _

   g. (obo miser) Protein producer: _ _ _ _ _ _ _ _ _

LS–3
Cells, Part 2

1. *What's Wrong?*: There are mistakes in each of the following sketches. Describe the problems on the lines under the sketches.

   a. **Plant Cell**

   cytoplasm
   centriole (8)
   nucleolus
   chlorophyll

   _____
   _____
   _____
   _____
   _____

   b. **Animal Cell**

   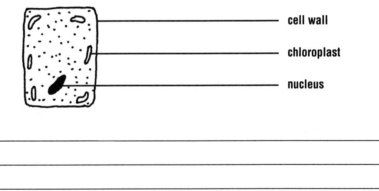

   cell wall
   chloroplast
   nucleus

   _____
   _____
   _____
   _____
   _____

2. *Cell Puzzle*: How many times can you spell cell with the container and letters without using any letter more than once? HINT: Reread the question.

   ```
   l   l
   c   c
   e   e
   l   l
   l   l
   e   e
   c   c
   c   c
   ```

   Cell can be spelled a total of _____ times.

LS–4
Cell Division

The duplication and division of the nucleus and the chromosomes during cell reproduction is known as mitosis.

IPMAT: The stages of mitosis are interphase, prophase, metaphase, anaphase, and telophase. What happens during each stage of cell reproduction? Combine the correct words from Column A with those of Column B to describe briefly what takes place in each stage of mitosis.

Column A	Column B
not, weak, resting, one	dividing, cell, complex, vacuole

— — — — — — — —   — — — — ; — — — — — — — — — — — — — —

INTERPHASE

thread, specialized, appear, homeostasis	chromosomes, nucleus, muscle, attack

— — — — — — — — — —   — — — — — —

PROPHASE

to, go, chromosome, break, hemoglobin, drop	up, pairs, occur, connective, join, line

— — — — — — — — — — —   — — — — — — — — — — — —

METAPHASE

respiration, chlorophyll, apart, group, plate	chromosomes, organ, split, chloroplast

— — — — — — — — — —   — — — — — — — — — —

ANAPHASE

form, six, none, body, law	cells, two, drop, arise, the

— — — — — — — — —   — — — — —

TELOPHASE

LS–5
Viruses

A virus is a microscopic substance that consists of either RNA or DNA. It relies on a specific host cell for its reproduction.

1. *True or False?*: There are three true statements about viruses below. Place a check mark (✔) on the line next to each true statement.

   ___ a.   A virus can be seen only with an electron microscope.

   ___ b.   A protein cover known as a capsid makes up a small part of a virus.

   ___ c.   A virus has several living structures within its capsid.

   ___ d.   Viruses can be spread via air, food, animals, and humans.

   ___ e.   A virus cannot reproduce outside of a living cell.

2. *Virus Attack*: Fill in the blanks with the letters that spell the names of diseases caused by viruses.

   <pre>
                        V
              _ o _ I _
                        R _ _ i e _
                     _ U _ _ s
              _ e _ S _ _ s
                        _ E _ m _ _   m _ a _ _ e _
              _ I _ S
   </pre>

3. *A Virus Appears*: Complete the following formula for making a virus.

   _ u _ l _ i _   a _ i _   +   _ r _ t _ i _   c _ a _   =   virus

4. *Just Kidding*: Ms. Bogus, biology teacher, told her class that no one can see viruses under an electron microscope. Ms. Bogus meant this as a joke. Describe the "humor" in her statement.

5. *Virus Riddle:* What do an inactive virus and a dormant volcano have in common?

LS–6
Monerans, Part 1

Monerans are simple, one-celled organisms. Bacteria are members of the Monera kingdom.

1. *Wrong Word*: Circle the word that makes each statement FALSE. Then write the correct word on the line.

   a. Oxygen-fixing bacteria help peanut plants build living material. _____

   b. Bacteria are one-celled animals. _____

   c. Bacteria can make their own food. _____

   d. Bacteria are classified according to their shape. The spirillum is rod-shaped. _____

   e. Most bacteria are harmful to humans. _____

   f. Some of the organisms in the Monera kingdom are bacteria. _____

   g. Bacteria reproduce by nuclear fission. _____

   h. Colds are caused by bacteria. _____

2. *Bacterial Buddies*: Some monerans recycle nutrients in the soil, provide nitrogen to plants, and help in food production. Shade in the letters in each row, from left to right, that spell the name of a dairy item produced with the help of bacteria. Their names rhyme with alert, sneeze, and flutter.

a.	e	c	g	h	a	t	p	e	b	e	i	s	o	l	r	e
b.	d	b	o	u	g	t	h	x	k	t	c	e	n	r	a	i
c.	p	e	a	y	s	n	o	g	a	u	b	r	o	e	t	i

   Bonus Question: What do you call the poisons some bacteria produce? They are called __ __ __ __ __ __. Combine TWO of the UNSHADED letters from each row—a, b, and c—to find the answer.

3. *Solve the Mysteries*: Tell what each of the following messages mean.

   a. c b a a f c e t t e e r r i i a a

   _____

   b. Nitrogen, N, Nitrogen, N, Nitrogen, N, Nitrogen, . . .

   _____

   c.

   _____

Name _____   Date _____

LS–7
Monerans, Part 2

1. *Terse Verse*: Complete the second line with a word that rhymes with the last word in the first line. All words relate to the life of bacteria.

   a.   If I'm to split with keen precision,
        Then make way for binary _ i _ s _ _ _.

   b.   I feed on dead things, day and night,
        So you can call me _ a _ r _ _ _ y _ _.

   c.   I have a cell wall, there's no escape;
        It helps me keep my beautiful _ _ a _ _.

   d.   When I feed, I do not loaf;
        Not this hungry _ e _ _ r _ t _ _ p _.

   e.   Because I have no way to sail,
        I energize my whiplike _ a _ _.

2. *Eight in a Crate*: Use the letters in the six boxes below to produce a term for the following statements. The eight letters in each box combine to form answers. Write the box number on the line to the left of the statement.

   ____ a.   A disease-causing moneran is known as a _ _ _ _ _ _ _ _ _.

   ____ b.   Spiral-shaped bacteria are known as _ _ _ _ _ _ _ _ _.

   ____ c.   A bacterium is a living _ _ _ _ _ _ _ _.

   ____ d.   Some bacteria have a whiplike structure that allows them to move
             about in the water. These structures are called _ _ _ _ _ _ _ _.

   ____ e.   Bacteria capable of producing toxins may cause a type of
             food poisoning called _ _ _ _ _ _ _ _.

   ____ f.   The bacterium responsible for causing botulism
             is the _ _ _ _ _ _ _ _.

1		2		3		4		5		6	
i	t	l	r	l	a	l	a	g	t	r	a
o	l	s	i	e	g	b	u	a	n	s	m
m	b	a	l	a	l	s	l	e	o	g	i
u	s	i	p	f	c	i	c	h	p	n	o

© 2001 by The Center for Applied Research in Education

LS–8
Protista

Organisms belonging to the kingdom Protista are mostly one-celled, animallike protozoans. Protists share characteristics found in both plants and animals. Protozoans are separated into four main groups based on their method of movement. These four groups are the sarcodines (amoeba), ciliates (paramecium), flagellates (euglena), and sporozoans (plasmodium). Amoebas slowly plod along extending their "false feet." Paramecia travel about by beating their tiny, hairlike cilia. The euglena relies on its whiplike tail to scurry around. Parasitic sporozoans depend on their hosts for transportation.

Protists Potpourri: There are 28 protozoan structures and characteristics listed below. They belong to the four protists shown in outline form. Place the number for each structure and/or characteristic belonging to the protist INSIDE the outline. Some numbers, of course, will match more than one protist.

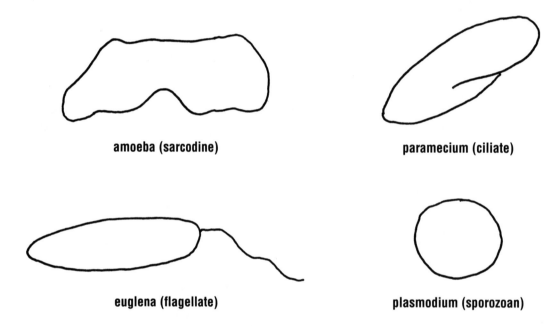

amoeba (sarcodine)   paramecium (ciliate)

euglena (flagellate)   plasmodium (sporozoan)

Structures and Characteristics

1. gullet	8. chloroplasts	15. micronucleus	22. unicellular
2. nucleus	9. autotroph	16. oral groove	23. slipper shape
3. pellicle	10. pseudopods	17. flagellum	24. has both plant/animal features
4. eyespot	11. contractile vacuole	18. binary fission (reproduction)	25. oval shape
5. heterotroph	12. cell membrane	19. conjugation (reproduction)	26. round shape
6. cytoplasm	13. cilia	20. indefinite shape	27. reproduces spores
7. food vacuole	14. macronucleus	21. parasitic forms	28. causes malaria

Name _____   Date _____

LS–9
Fungi

Fungi, plural for fungus, are not plants. They are placed in a separate kingdom. Plants, of course, are members of the plant kingdom; fungi belong to the fungi kingdom.

1. *What's Missing?*: Unscramble the jumbled letters to learn why fungi are not classified as plants.

    a. Fungi are unable to (kaem) _____ (hiter) _____ (now) _____ (dofo) _____.

    b. (lryhlcoploh) _____ is not present in fungi.

2. *You Are What You Eat*: Some organisms feast upon dead materials. A fungus is an example. Organisms that do this are given a certain name. Use all the letters in the three words to produce the answer.

    prop   as   they

    A fungus is a __ __ __ __ __ __ __ __ __.

3. *Fungi Alumni*: The words below rhyme with the names of several different fungi. Write the name of each fungus on the line next to the rhyming words.

    a. bold, scold, told   _____

    b. coral, whorl, laurel   _____

    c. undo, redo, greenish-blue   _____

    d. busts, gusts, musts   _____

    e. huts, cuts, nuts   _____

    f. beasts, feasts   _____

4. *The Fun in Fungus*: It never fails. Whenever Mr. O. Shumo, fungi expert, gives a talk on fungi, the class breaks out into laughter when he is introduced to the audience. Why do you think the crowd laughs? HINT: Name an edible fungus. The NAME's the SAME.

5. *Dark Side*: A fungus may be harmful to plants or animals. Athlete's foot and ringworm are examples of problems for people. What do you call a fungus that lives on or in the bodies of other organisms? Unscramble the letters and symbol for the answer.

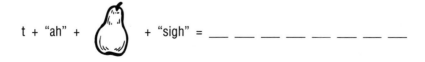

t + "ah" +   + "sigh" = __ __ __ __ __ __ __ __

73

LS–10
Plants, Part 1

A vascular plant has transporting tubes that carry materials throughout the plant. Let's look at some of these plants and their main features.

1. *A Tube or Two*: The diagram below represents a plant with five branches. Draw a series of transporting tubes throughout the plant.

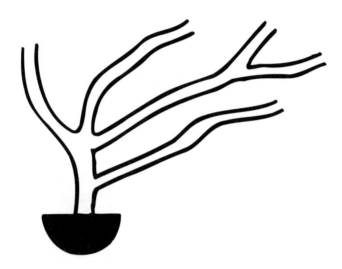

2. *Add Some Stems and Leaves, Too*: A vascular plant has stems, leaves, and roots. The roots in the plant above are buried in potting soil. Go ahead and draw some leaves and stems on the plant diagram. Do not darken or shade in the leaves and stems. Now sketch a series of transporting tubes extending into the leaves and stems.

3. *Vascular Search*: As you know, a vascular plant has leaves, stems, and roots. Circle eight common vascular plants in the leaf outline below.

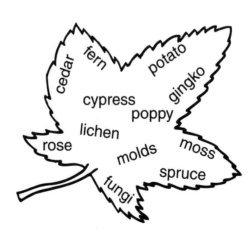

Name _____   Date _____

LS–11
Plants, Part 2

1. *Two-Clue Plant Terms*: Use the clues to help you identify the plant features or structures.

Feature or Structure   **Two-Word Clue**

a.   _ y _ e _   water, carrier
b.   _ _ n o _ _ _   cotyledon, one
c.   _ t _ m _ _ _   openings, leaf
d.   p _ _ _ i _   flower, female
e.   _ _ n i _ _ _   "cone-bearer"
f.   f _ _ n _ _   leaves, fern
g.   _ _ m _ o _ p _ _ m _   seeds, uncovered
h.   _ e _ _   ovule, fertilized
i.   p _ _ o _ _   food, carrier
j.   a _ g _ o _ _ e _ _ _   plants, flowers
k.   _ e t _ _ _ _   leaf, stalk
l.   _ _ _ t   plant, anchor
m.   _ r _ _ _   seeds, ovary
n.   _ e _ a _ _   protection, petals
o.   _ t _ m _ _   male, flower
p.   c _ _ _   cells, bark

2. *Silly Puzzlers from the Plant World:*

   a.   If a flea wanted to change into a leaf, what would it have to do?

   b.   What do the illustrations represent?

   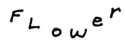

   c.   What does this letter arrangement represent?

   r   o
   o   t

   d.   If a dicot is a seed with two cotyledons and a monocot is a seed with only one cotyledon, what is an apricot?

   e.   If a bunch of carrots attended a basketball game, what would they form?

   f.   Sepals surround and protect the petals in a flower. Show, by rearranging letters, how a sepal makes up 80 percent of a petal.

LS–12
Plants, Part 3

1. *We Need Plants*: This is an understatement. We depend on plants for food, shelter, clothing, decoration, and oxygen. We couldn't survive without plants. Locate and circle 12 plants in the puzzle. Then write their names in alphabetical order in the space under the puzzle. Answers may be up, down, forward, backward, or diagonal.

```
n  e  d  q  f  z  j  o  u
o  t  a  e  h  w  a  y  g
t  x  r  g  f  k  h  v  r
t  n  d  i  l  e  u  i  a
o  e  r  o  m  a  c  y  s
c  q  j  p  x  e  a  d  s
b  l  i  p  a  m  j  z  u
```

2. *Love Those Plants*: Write the names of two plants (not mentioned in Part 1 above) that serve as examples for each of the areas beneficial to humans.

   a. food   _____ and _____

   b. shelter   _____ and _____

   c. clothing   _____ and _____

   d. decoration   _____ and _____

   e. medicine   _____ and _____

   f. oxygen   _____ and _____

3. *Eat Your Vegetables*: Yum. Edible plants. Now's your chance to find six mouth-watering vegetables in the statements below. The letters needed to spell each vegetable may be mixed or appear forward or backward. Circle the vegetable and write its name on the line next to the statement.

   a. "No, No. I can't east those!"   _____

   b. How rad is Harold's car?   _____

   c. Cheryl's pet bee, Toby, flew away.   _____

   d. Let cute Mary go with us.   _____

   e. May I go shopping with you?   _____

   f. "Ok, rabbit. Come out of your hole."   _____

Name _____   Date _____

LS–13
Simple Invertebrates: Sponges

A sponge is a simple, aquatic animal with a porous structure. All sponges belong to the phylum Porifera. Porifera means "pore-bearer."

1. *Sponge or Rock?*: Sketch A and Sketch B are nearly identical. Each could be a sponge or a rock. Use your artistic talent to turn both of them into sponges.

A   **B**

2. *Three-Letter Search*: Twelve terms related to various features of a sponge appear below. Each term is missing three letters. Fill in the blanks with the missing letters.

Sponge Features		**Term**
a.	This moves through sponge	_ a _ e _
b.	Fabricated sponge	s _ n t _ e _ i c
c.	Food and water intake	_ o _ _ s
d.	Replace lost parts	r _ _ e n e _ a t e
e.	Supports body	_ p i _ u _ e
f.	No backbone	s _ i n _ l e s s
g.	Remains attached	s e _ _ i _ e
h.	Taillike structures	f l _ _ e l _ a
i.	Bud reproduction	_ s e _ _ a l
j.	Inside body cells	c _ l _ a _
k.	Absent in sponges	o r _ _ _ s
l.	Large openings	_ s c _ l a

3. *Sponge Riddles*:
   a. Where would you find the largest hole in a sponge?

   b. Why did the mother porifera toss her oldest son out of the colony?

LS–14
Simple Invertebrates: Corals and Sea Anemones

Corals and sea anemones belong to the phylum Cnidaria. They, like sponges, are simple animals that live in the ocean.

1. *Coral Collection*: Use the clues to find five things associated with coral.

	Clues
_ **C** _ _ _	aqueous abode
_ **O** _ _ _	soft-bodied organism
R _ _ _	coral colony clutter
A _ _ _ _	half-moon around the lagoon
_ _ _ _ **L** _ _	rings and things

2. *Coral Condo*: Skeletons of dead coral pile up and form coral reefs. The reef's outer layer contains living corals.

    A coral __ __ __ __ p has tentacles surrounding its mouth. The tentacles help trap tasty morsels for it to eat.

    Unscramble the circled letters to find the missing word.

3. *Sea Flower*: Unscramble the letters in parentheses and write the words in the blanks.

    Sea anemones use their _____ (centslate) to

    _____ (trapeuc) passing fish. They use _____

    (gnitngis) _____ (lecsl) to _____ (opnosi)

    the fish.

4. *Roundup*: Circle the items below that relate to BOTH coral and sea anemones.

tentacles	live alone	outer skeleton
ligaments	marine	live in colonies
soft-bodied	central cavity	Aurelia
teeth	autotroph	polyps
mouth	reef	spicule

LS–15
Simple Invertebrates: Hydras and Jellyfish

Two more members of the phylum Cnidaria are hydras and jellyfish. There is a mix of statements below regarding hydras and jellyfish. Eight of them are false. Circle the letter preceding each false statement.

1. *Eight Untruths*

   a. A hydra is a multicellular organism.
   b. A jellyfish goes through a sessile medusa stage.
   c. Hydras use a whiplike tail for locomotion.
   d. Hydras undergo budding to reproduce themselves.
   e. Medusa is the nonswimming form of a jellyfish.
   f. Hydras live in salty ponds and marshes.
   g. Jellyfish tentacles have stinging cells.
   h. Many holes or pores line the surface of a jellyfish.

   i. Jellyfish drift about on the surface of the ocean.
   j. Hydras are sessile animals; they can't move around.
   k. Jellyfish are known as coelenterates.
   l. Hydras have only one body opening.
   m. The polyp is the sexual generation of a jellyfish.
   n. Hydras use tentacles to capture food.
   o. Jellyfish use muscle tissue to move about in the water.
   p. Hydras reproduce by binary fission.

2. *A Conversation Between Coelenterates*: A jellyfish is NOT a fish. It's a free-swimming creature shaped like an umbrella. Complete the following dialogue between two cnidarians.

   JOE JELLYFISH: "You know, Moe, I'd really like to become a fish."

   MOE JELLYFISH: "Sure. What do you have to lose?"

   JOE JELLYFISH: "_____."

3. *Three on a Spree*: Simple invertebrates are animals with few body parts. They do not have backbones. Three of the following animals are hidden in the puzzle: coral, sea anemone, hydra, sponge, jellyfish. Shade in the letters that spell the three names. They may appear forward, backward, up, or down.

e	a	e	s	f	r	o	c	e	y	f	i	s
l	a	o	y	i	a	e	a	r	l	o	s	p
a	n	e	m	s	l	■	g	d	l	■	h	o
h	i	r	o	h	■	e	l	y	e	c	■	n
s	■	e	n	s	■	■	h	j	a	■	g	

The darkened area will reveal the answer to this question: Where do the animals in the puzzle live?

They live _____.

LS–16
Worms

Worms are more than "little slimy wigglies." The worm world produces a variety of organisms with various shapes, sizes, and behavioral patterns. How much do you know about these animals?

1. *Worm Smart*: Match the worms in the left column with their related features in the right column. Each worm will have five or more features. Write the numbers on the line.

Worm		Worm Features
a. tapeworm	_____	1. platyhelminthes
b. leech	_____	2. soft-bodied
c. earthworm	_____	3. annelids
d. planarian	_____	4. bilateral symmetry
e. hookworm	_____	5. lives on land or in water
f. trichina	_____	6. round body
g. ascaris	_____	7. free-living
h. fluke	_____	8. parasitic
i. featherduster	_____	9. flat shape
j. heartworm	_____	10. lives in salt water
k. bloodworm	_____	11. segmented body
l. arrow worm	_____	12. nemahelminthes
		13. lives in the soil
		14. lives in fresh water
		15. undercooked meat

2. *Parasitic Critic*: Use the rhyming clues to identify the parasitic worms below.

    a.   You only need a single tip:
            Search below the lower lip.

            Parasitic worm: _____

    b.   An athletic trainer's basic need—
            a part of this worm? Yes, indeed!

            Parasitic worm: _____

    c.   Tissue damage leaves many signs;
            this parasite may be found in swines.

            Parasitic worm: _____

LS–17
More Worms

Here's another opportunity to put a worm in its place. Use the clues in the descriptions below to identify four parasites and one free-living worm.

1. I'm in pretty good SHAPE; I've been A-ROUND,
   and humans are the final hosts.
   This nematode should hit the road.
   A muscle home? The cyst will insist.
   I "dig" Mr. Pig. So treat the meat before you eat.

   — — — — — — — __ worm

2. I'm a SUCKER for a good-looking host.
   I'm a parasite, all right.
   In years past, a medicinal blast.
   I like a plasma cuisine; I'm a nematode supreme.

   — — — — —

3. Resembles a leaf, this liver thief.
   Let's not pretend, my friend; raw fish should
      not be your dish.
   What do I enjoy the most? Perhaps an attachment
      to a host.
   I go a-huntin' for wool-covered mutton.

   — — — — —   — — — — —   — — — — —

4. Suckers and hooks give me my looks.
   A parasite, both day and night,
      my shape led to my name.
   I'd trade a scolex for a Rolex.
   A primate appears in my name.

   — — — — — — — —

5. With over one hundred body segments,
   I'm watching out for the "early bird."
   Light and rain, they drive me insane.
   I'm round and long, but no King Kong.
   I have an "ear," but cannot hear.

   — — — — — — — — —

LS–18
Mollusks

1. Mollusks are soft-bodied organisms that are often covered by a shell. Two examples are clams and snails. Use the group of three rhyming words to help you find five more mollusks.

Three Rhyming Words	Mollusks
mug, dug, rug	__ __ __ g
rib, kid, bid	__ __ __ i __
frighten, Titan, heighten	__ h __ __ __ __
armpit, unfit, culprit	__ __ __ p __ __
phony, ceremony, rigatoni	__ __ a __ __ __ __

2. Use the following descriptive statements to draw a typical mollusk in the box.
   - flat, muscular foot located below shell
   - a spiral-shaped shell
   - a body with a head at one end (eye, mouth, tentacle) and anus at the other end; the body lies between the shell and foot

3. Two snails entered a race. They decided to crawl a distance of 12 inches. Snail A moved one foot (30.48 cm) in 6.1 minutes. Snail B made it to the halfway point as Snail A crossed the finish line. At this pace, what would Snail B move in 12.2 minutes? (**Warning:** A trick lies ahead!)

4. Circle the mollusk-related item in each sentence below.
   a. Aren't boys terrible?
   b. Carol's luggage got lost at the airport.
   c. Bambi Valveoni is the best female athlete in school.
   d. Helen's nail got caught in her wool sweater.
   e. Mr. C. hit one ball from the tee to the green.

5. *Bonus Problems:*
   a. Identify this tall, pointed gastropod from the North American seas. Its name rhymes with logger and jogger. This shell, with many twists, is an __ __ g __ __.
   b. Where would you find most of the murky marshy mollusk mussel's muscle? *Answer:* In the animal's __ __ __ __.
   c. What would a snail have to lose in order to resemble the slug? It would have to lose its __ __ __ __ __.

© 2001 by The Center for Applied Research in Education

LS–19
Echinoderms

1. Echinoderms have rough, spiny skins. Replace the words in parentheses with the REAL name given to each echinoderm.

   sea (sun)   __ __ a __
   sea (mischievous boy)   __ r __ __ __ __
   sea ("pickle")   __ __ __ __ m __ __ __
   sand (peso)   __ __ __ __ a __
   sea (hyacinth)   __ __ __ y

2. Echinoderms have an internal skeleton made up of spines. The letters *o, d, e, n* produce the name of this "inside" skeleton when arranged in their proper order. It isn't enod or done or node. So what else could it be?

   That's easy. It's an __ __ __ __skeleton.

3. Use the words in the box below to fill in the blanks for each statement.

   a. Echinoderms live only in the __ __ __ __ __.

   b. Echinoderms have a __ __ __ __ __ __ symmetry.

   c. Sea cucumbers lack __ __ __ __.

   d. Sea urchins move by means of their stalked __ __ __ __ feet and by means of their __ __ __ __ __ __.

   e. Echinoderms may __ __ __ __ __ __ __ a lost or injured body part.

   f. Echinoderms have a __ __ __ __ __ - vascular system to help them move, feed, get oxygen, and dispose of wastes.

river	ocean	replace
remove	spines	radial
simple	teeth	vapor
skin	feet	blood
water	lungs	tube

4. *Brain Twister:* Why can't you believe anything a sea cucumber says?

LS–20
Arthropods

Arthropods are joint-legged animals. They represent the largest animal phylum. Arthropods have segmented bodies and carry around an external skeleton.

1. Eight arthropods appear below. Two imposters are hiding in the group of animals. Expose the frauds by circling them.

tarantula	crayfish	scorpion	tick	gastropod
nautilus	cicada	isopod	bee	lobster

2. What do you call the outside covering of an arthropod? Put these clues together for the answer.

    e + x + o + 206 human bones = __ __ __ __ __ __ __ __ __ __ __ __

3. Arthropods are invertebrates with jointed legs. Find the mystery arthropod with 34 body segments and 68 legs among the group of animals listed below. Circle the mystery critter.

pillbug	millipede	cricket	lobster
cicada	barnacle	scorpion	black widow
crayfish	centipede	mite	grasshopper

4. The hard, outside shell of an arthropod is made of a substance called chitin. Use the letters in CHITIN to help reveal the body structures and features of arthropods.

	Clues
C _ _ _ _ _ _ _ _ _	open system
H _ _ _	anterior body part
_ _ _ I _ _	all are segmented
T _ _ _ _ _	from head to abdomen
_ _ _ _ I _ _	shedding outside shell
_ _ _ _ N _ _ _ _	external organ

LS–21
Arthropods: Arachnids

Spiders, scorpions, mites, and ticks are members of the Class Arachnoidea. These animals have various body shapes and appendages. Some are harmful to people, but most of them are quite harmless.

1. *Arachnid Puzzle*: Use the clues to help you complete the puzzle of arachnid characteristics.

ACROSS:
2. tick food
3. number of body parts
5. some live on insects
6. eyes that see changes in light
8. spiders spin webs with these
9. number of spider legs
11. spider food

DOWN:
1. a body segment
4. number of appendages (2 words)
7. a scorpion's home
10. transmits Lyme disease

2. *Spider Riddles*:

a. Where would you find a spider with eight scattered legs and a disconnected body?

b. A spider has eight simple eyes. Where would you find one main eye?

LS–22
Arthropods: Crustaceans

Shrimp, crayfish, crabs, and lobsters are the main members of the Class Crustacea. These animals live in or around water.

1. *A Crustacean Carnival*: The information needed to complete each statement below can be found in the puzzle. Circle the answers and place them in the appropriate spaces. Answers may be up, down, forward, backward, or diagonal.

   a. A hermit crab's home is often an empty _____.

   b. A crustacean uses _____ to obtain oxygen from water.

   c. Crustaceans can _____ or replace lost body parts.

   d. A crustacean uses its _____ to crush food.

   e. A pillbug lives in a _____ environment.

   f. _____ can be found on a crustacean's first pair of legs.

   g. A crustacean known as a _____ lives stuck to boat and piers.

   h. A crayfish uses _____ for movement and reproduction.

   i. The cover for the head-chest area of a crayfish is called a

      _____.

   j. Crustaceans known as _____ provide a main source of food for whales.

   k. A crayfish has _____ main body parts.

   l. Crustaceans use _____ as sense organs for taste and touch.

   m. A lobster and crayfish see with _____ eyes.

   n. Crustaceans have _____ or more pairs of legs.

```
m  s  w  i  m  m  e  r  e  t  s  f  p
a  k  w  c  j  d  n  u  o  p  m  o  c
x  r  o  a  c  a  r  a  p  a  c  e  f
i  i  g  n  j  s  l  l  i  g  b  i  o
l  l  e  l  c  a  n  r  a  b  v  w  q
a  l  e  l  h  e  a  n  n  e  t  n  a
d  x  a  e  t  a  r  e  n  e  g  e  r
i  w  m  l  v  m  o  i  s  t  u  r  a
s  i  m  p  l  e  t  k  l  l  e  h  s
```

2. *Crustacean Riddle*: What part of a crustacean shows the greatest amount of inactivity?

© 2001 by The Center for Applied Research in Education

Name _____   Date _____

LS–23
Arthropods: Centipedes and Millipedes

The centipede belongs in the Class Chilopoda. The millipede is a member of the Class Diplopoda. One of these animals can inflict a painful bite. Do you know which one?

1. *Create a Centipede*: Use the following description to sketch a centipede in the box.

   - Has a head; one pair of antennae
   - Flat, wormlike body
   - One pair of legs per body segment
   - Has jointed legs

2. *Make a Millipede*: Use the following description to sketch a millipede in the box.

   - Has a head; one pair of antennae
   - Round, wormlike body
   - Two pairs of legs per body segment
   - Has jointed legs

3. *Problem: Which One Bites?*

   Here's a clue:

   The one with the "lip" treats you right;
   But the "tip"? No. He likes to bite.

   Answer: The _____ likes to bite.

LS–24
Arthropods: Insects

Insects comprise the largest group of arthropods. They have jointed legs, three body sections, and six legs. Many of them have wings and antennae.

1. *Generic Insect*: The figure below represents the body of an insect. A list of insect structures are located under the figure. Place the letter identifying each structure on or around the figure where they normally appear on an insect.

head

© 2001 by The Center for Applied Research in Education

a. thorax	f. abdomen
b. first pair of legs	g. antennae
c. second pair of legs	h. compound eye
d. third pair of legs	i. hindwing
e. forewing	j. exoskeleton

2. *So You Think You Know Insects*: Here's a chance to test your expertise. Circle the three non-insects listed below. One is hiding in each group.

chiton	sow bug	termite
bristletail	springtail	pillbug
skipper	mealybug	mayfly
froghopper	darner	ichneumon
mantid	chalcid	skimmer

3. *Insect Puzzler*: How many different insect names can you spell with the following letters? List them on the lines below. Be on the lookout for a trick.

B   E   E
T   L   E

Answer: How many? _____ (number)

_____

LS–25
Arthropods: More Insects

1. Mr. Hopper, science teacher, wrote five words on the board: hoe   max   bat   dead   horn. He said, "OK, class, you have one minute to use ALL of the letters in these words to write the three main body parts of a dragonfly." Try it. See if you can break the one-minute barrier.

2. Circle the insect that matches the rhymed clues.

   a. There's a chance you don't suspect,
      my name carries a non-insect.

      termite   mealybug   aphid   cricket

   b. Dairy product in the air . . .
      Silly? Sure, but I don't care.

      cicada   butterfly   mantid   wasp

   c. If I stop short, it's part of the game;
      So "quit" I shall, if it's all the same.

      mayfly   midge   mosquito   beetle

   d. When you're "counting sheep" at night,
      I'll crawl about and take a bite.

      moth   sawfly   bedbug   no-see-um

   e. You'll hear my "song" but shan't see me;
      much of the time I'm high in the tree.

      cicada   leafhopper   horsefly   treehopper

   f. I show pretty colors, no one dare deny;
      I'll be eating aphids till the day I die.

      lacewing   damselfly   midge   ladybug

3. Add the total number of insects: 3 ticks, 8 sow bugs, 2 mites, 4 pillbugs, and 5 bristletails. How many did you count? The number of insects is _____.

4. *Insect Riddle:* What do you call an insect without wings?

5. *Insect Puzzler:* A cricket and a tick wanted to see the flea circus. They didn't have any money so they combined resources and gained admission. How did they do this?

Name _____   Date _____

LS–26
Vertebrates

Vertebrates are animals with backbones. Some of their features include an internal skeleton of bone and/or cartilage, a well-developed nervous system with a brain and spinal cord, and a complex sensory system. Use the two-word clues to help you identify several vertebrate members of the phylum Chordata.

	Vertebrate	Two-Word Clue
1.	_ _ _ **A**	canned fish
2.	**V** _ _ _ _	venomous snake
3.	_ _ _ **E** _ _	park, bird
4.	_ _ _ _ **R** _ _ _	tree, rodent
5.	_ _ _ _ _ **T** _	elephant, extinct
6.	_ _ _ **E** _	insectivore, molelike
7.	_ _ **B** _ _	bird, breast
8.	_ _ _ **R** _ _	"fish hawk"
9.	_ _ _ **A** _ _ _	"cow," flippers
10.	_ _ _ **T** _ _ _ _	turtle, land
11.	_ _ _ _ _ **E** _ _	large, caviar
12.	_ **H** _ _ _	Africa, horns
13.	_ **A** _ _ _ _	migrates, chinook
14.	_ _ **S** _ _	ruminant, bovid
15.	_ _ _ **A** _ _ _ _	food, tuna
16.	_ _ _ **N** _	wolflike, Africa
17.	_ **E** _ _ _	shiner, fish
18.	_ _ **R** _ _ _ _	primate, vegetarian
19.	**V** _ _ _ _ _ _ _	prey, bird
20.	_ _ _ **E**	northern, fish
21.	_ _ _ **C** _ _ _ _ _	rodent, quills
22.	_ _ _ _ **O** _ _	carnivore, bands
23.	_ _ **R** _	snowshoe, Canada
24.	_ _ _ **D** _ _ _ _ _	wood, bird

Vertebrate Puzzler: Use the letters in VERTEBRATE to identify three more *vertebrates*. You may use a letter more than once.

They are _____, _____, and

_____.

90

© 2001 by The Center for Applied Research in Education

LS–27
Vertebrates: Fish, Part 1

1. *Missing Parts*: The outline below represents a bony fish with eight missing structures. Sketch the following features on the outline: eye, nostril, pectoral fin, pelvic fin, dorsal fin, anal fin, caudal fin, and body scales.

2. *Match 'Em*: Match the fish structure with its function. Write the number of the function on the line. Some answers may be used more than once; other may not apply.

Structure		Function
a. caudal fin	_____	1. serves as sensory organ
b. operculum	_____	2. smell; detects odors
c. gills	_____	3. propels or paddles
d. lateral line	_____	4. covers the gills
e. pectoral fin	_____	5. helps to stabilize
f. pelvic fin	_____	6. protection
g. anal fin	_____	7. swimming, steering
h. dorsal fin	_____	8. breathing
i. body scales	_____	9. circulates blood
		10. stimulates aortic arches

3. *Go Figure*: To answer both questions correctly, make no mistakes with the math calculations located in parentheses. Circle the matching answer for each question.

   a. How many heart chambers does a bony fish have?

   1   2   3   4   5

   (Multiply 240 by three. Take away 680 from the answer. Divide the remaining number by the sum of 4 + 8 + 8.)

   b. How many pairs of cranial nerves does a bony fish have?

   4   5   7   8   10

   (Divide 4.5 by 15. Times this answer by 30. Add 1 to the last answer.)

LS–28
Vertebrates: Fish, Part 2

1. *Find the Right Letters:* Sharks and rays have skeletons made of __ __ __ __ __ b __ __ c __ r __ __ __ __ __ __. Use the letters in EXIT and FLAG to fill in the blanks. You may use a letter more than once.

2. *Clear for Takeoff:* Flying fish are known to glide through the air up to 100 feet or more. What body feature allows them to fly? Use ANY of the following six letters to spell the answer:

   f   n   w   i   s   g

3. *Vanishing Fish:* Some desirable species of fish have declined over the years. To show this problem, use ONE word from Group A and ONE word from Group B to complete the following illustration:

   There's a fish
   decline because . . .

   (A) __ __ __ __ __ __
   (B) __ __ __ __

   Group A: wastes, sewage, grease, humans, litter

   Group B: gunk, oils, fish, dirt, nets

4. *Baked, Fried, or Poached?:* You've heard horror stories about sharks attacking surfers and swimmers. Write a FOUR-WORD description of a man-eating fish. You MUST use only the words in the box. You may not use the same word twice. Watch out! A trick swims about.

leg	sandwich	man
seal	diver	tuna
eating	predator	orca
teeth	smell	attack

5. *Fish Puzzler #1:* How is it possible to catch 20 sea perch on a single hook at the same time?

6. *Fish Puzzler #2:* Myrna bragged that she hooked and played a 22-pound salmon for 15 minutes. Unfortunately, the fish broke her line and got away. If the fish escaped, how did she know how much it weighed?

LS–29
Vertebrates: Amphibians

1. Most amphibians have moist skin, webbed feet, and no claws. They use gills, lungs, and skin for respiration. *Examples:* salamanders, toads, and frogs. See how many amphibians you can identify from the clues in the rhyming lines.

   a. I have no legs and cannot see,
      So won't you please take care of me?

      _ a _ _   _ a _ a _ a _ _ _ _   (2 words)

   b. I'm a "waterdog" to those in the south,
      With plumelike gills at the side of my mouth.

      _ u _ _ u _ _ _

   c. A twig or branch, just take your pick;
      Who really cares? I'm built to stick.

      _ r _ _ _ r _ _

   d. I'm chunky and short with warty skin,
      I live on land and the frog's my kin.

      _ _ _ _

2. Amphibians are classified in the phylum Chordata. Fill in the spaces with letters that spell the names of eight different amphibians.

   _ _ _ **C** _ _ _ _ _

   h _ _ _ _ _ _ _ _ _

   _ **o** _ _

   _ _ **r** _ _

   _ _ **d** _ _ _ _

   _ _ _ _ **a** _ _   frog

   _ _ _ **t**

   a _ _ _ _ _ _

3. Amphibians live part of the time on land and part of the time in _ _ _ _ _. How can you use "HOH" to complete the sentence?

4. *Amphibian Puzzlers:* Decode the following messages:

   a. S A L t A c M e A s N n D i E R
      ◄—————————

   b. h T i H b E e   W r I n N a T t E e R

© 2001 by The Center for Applied Research in Education

LS–30
Vertebrates: Reptiles

1. Reptiles are vertebrates with dry, scaly skin. Some have feet with claws. Identify three reptiles from these clues:

Clues	Reptile
a. beautifully colored; venomous; a "monster"	a. _ i _ Ⓞ _ _ n _ Ⓞ _ _
b. a turtle; lives on land	b. _ o _ _ _ _ _ e
c. large snake; a crusher	c. Ⓞ _ _ _ o Ⓞ

Bonus Item: Use the circled letters to spell the name of an Australian poisonous snake. _ _ i _ a _

2. Correct the following false statements in four or fewer words.
    a. Beverly owns a four-legged tree snake.
    _____

    b. Reptiles have a two- or three-chambered heart.
    _____

    c. Reptiles are warm-blooded invertebrates.
    _____

    d. The head of a crocodile is broad and rounded.
    _____

    e. Cold-blooded reptiles thrive in dry, polar climates.
    _____

    f. Tortoises spend most of their lives in water.
    _____

3. *Reptile Puzzlers*:
    a. Why are young reptiles unimpressed when they hear, "Gee, you look just like your parents?"

    b. Most reptiles lead active lives. "Activity" means being active. What 9-letter word that contains "tivity" spells disaster for some reptiles?

    c. The mighty reptile T. rex stood 18 feet tall. Where would a two-foot mammal appear higher?

4. *Reptilian Riddle*: What lizard is mostly skin?

LS–31
Vertebrates: Birds

1. Use four of the words below to fill in the blanks. HINT: Make compound words. Birds have a spine, two pairs of limbs, and feathers. They also are warm-blooded, have a _ _ _ _ _ _ _ _ _ _ beak and _ _ _ _ _ _ _ _ _ _ _ _ bones.

solid	less	sacs	light	bill
colored	weight	hair	tooth	claws

2. How many bird claws can you construct from the groups of letters below? HINT: What's another name for a bird claw?

o	k	a	c	a	b	c
n	w	c	l	w	l	a
a	l	w	a	e	a	l
c	a	l	w	w	o	t

3. Fill in the blanks with any of the scattered letters. You may use a letter more than once. Birds also reproduce _ _ _ _ _ _ _ _ and have a _ _ _ _ _ _ _ _ _.

   b   u   o   e   k   y

       l   n   c   a   s   x

4. Look at the bird names strung together. Circle the three names of animals that do not belong in the bird kingdom.

   a. wrensparrowwoodpeckergooseroachpigeonospreywigeon

   b. owlpeweeoriolevireotealwilletcaimanbitternwarbler

   c. loongrousekilldeergrebemudskippercootgracklefinch

5. *Bird Puzzlers*:

   a. Don't bring up the subject of birds around Mel Gumpa. He brags that he's responsible for ALL the feathers on a bird. Weird? Perhaps, but what does he mean?

   b. A bird's body can be divided into a head, neck, trunk, and tail. Use four letters to indicate the four parts of a bird. (A trick? It's okay to think there might be.)

6. *Bird Riddles*:

   a. Why do some birds fly lower than other birds?

   b. Who brings gifts to birds at Christmas time?

LS–32
Vertebrates: Mammals, Part 1

Mammals are well-developed animals with these characteristics:

- Body usually covered with hair or fur.
- They have a four-chambered heart.
- Their warm-blooded body temperature remains fairly constant.
- Young drink milk from their mother's mammary glands.
- Most mammals experience live birth.
- Most mammals have a large, well-developed brain.

1. Match the animal with its description. Place the number opposite the description on the line.

Mammal		**Description**
_____ a.	chipmunk	1. sirenian, Florida
_____ b.	sea lion	2. territorial, stripes
_____ c.	walrus	3. hoofed, reindeer
_____ d.	armadillo	4. downward tusks
_____ e.	sea otter	5. puma, mountains
_____ f.	shrew	6. pouch, marsupial
_____ g.	woodchuck	7. barks, performs
_____ h.	whale	8. fishlike, blowhole
_____ i.	caribou	9. "wildcat," spots
_____ j.	bison	10. squirrel, chunky
_____ k.	elephant seal	11. wings, cave
_____ l.	wolverine	12. weasel family
_____ m.	peccary	13. omnivore, musk
_____ n.	opossum	14. back swimmer
_____ o.	narwhal	15. slim, molelike
_____ p.	mountain lion	16. largest pinniped
_____ q.	moose	17. largest rodent
_____ r.	prairie dog	18. groundhog, marmot
_____ s.	beaver	19. aquatic, tusk
_____ t.	bobcat	20. edentate, armor
_____ u.	skunk	21. enormous, hump
_____ v.	bat	22. wild pig
_____ w.	manatee	23. largest deer

(continued)

LS–32 (continued)

2. *Mammal Riddles*:

    a.   What do you call a 200-year American buffalo celebration?

    b.   Why did Robert Feline hate to go to school?

    c.   Who needs to protect the manatee population?

LS–33
Vertebrates: Mammals, Part 2

1. All mammals have certain characteristics that set them apart from other living things. Use ALL the letters from the words in parentheses to fill in the empty spaces.

a. Mammals are _ _ _ _-_ l _ _ _ _ _.
   (ram, wood, bed)

b. They have a f _ _ _-_ _ _ m _ _ _ _ _ _ _ _ _ _.
   (breed, art, hour, ache)

c. Mammals have _ o _ _   h _ _ _.
   (day, rib)

d. They are highly _ _ _ _ l _ i _ _ _ _.
   (tin, gentle)

e. Mammals feed their young with milk produced in _ _ _ _ _ _ _ _   _ _ _ n d _.
   (yam, gram, slam)

2. Cross out the letters needed to spell "mammals" below. The remaining letters spell the name of a mystery mammal. What is it?

    m   s   a   m
    m   a   l   l
    a   m   l   a

The mystery beast of burden is a _ _ _ _ _.

3. Migration is an example of a behavior _ _ _ _ _ _ _ in mammals. The designs below will give you a clue to the missing word. HINT: Something to be imitated.

    b   e   h   a   b   h   v   o
                    or
    v   i   o   r   e   a   i   r

4. All of these mammals begin with the letter **m**. Use the clues to help you find the answers. Write your answers in the spaces provided.

Mammals	Clues
a. _ _ _ _ _ _ _	feline, no tail
b. _ _ _ _ _ _ _ _	monkey family; very small
c. _ _ _ _ _	large deer; huge antlers
d. _ _ _ _ _ _ _	rodent, musklike odor
e. _ _ _ _ _ _ _	known as a sea cow
f. _ _ _ _ _ _ _	woolly, extinct
g. _ _ _ _ _ _ _ _	carnivore, kills snakes

LS–34
Human Skeletal System, Part 1

The human skeletal system is made of bone and cartilage. The skeletal system provides protection for vital organs, gives a body shape, and holds it together.

1. *Skeletal Survey*:

   a. Darken the answers to the items below in the puzzle. Write the answers in the empty spaces to the right of the descriptions.

Known as a shin bone	_ _ _ _ _
Forearm bone, thumb side	_ _ _ _ _ _
Also called a kneecap	_ _ _ _ _ _ _
The skull	_ _ _ _ _ _ _
Below the thoracic region	_ _ _ _ _ _
Bone between knee and ankle	_ _ _ _ _ _
The shoulder blade	_ _ _ _ _ _ _

   b. Draw a line through the letters in the puzzle that spell the answers to these questions:

      What is another name for the "funny bone"?

      What bone are you resting on when you sit?

   c. *Mystery Question:* Unscramble the remaining letters in the puzzle to answer this question:

      What is the name of the flat, uppermost pelvic bone?

      The name of the bone is the _____.

h	t	r	f	p	s	c	l	i
u	i	a	i	a	c	r	u	s
m	b	d	b	t	a	a	m	c
e	i	i	u	e	p	n	b	h
r	a	u	l	l	u	i	a	i
u	i	s	a	l	l	u	r	u
s	m	l	u	a	a	m	i	m

2. *Bone Connection*: Bones meet at a joint. Use the clues to help you name four types of movable joints in the body.

   ```
                J
        _ _ _ O _ _ _        side-to-side movement
          _ I _ _ _          movement in one direction
        _ _ _ _ _ N _        sliding movement
        _ _ _ _ _ T          ball and (?)
                S
   ```

LS–35
Human Skeletal System, Part 2

1. How many bones does the skull contain? To find out, do the following math:

    Add one dozen to six pair. Then subtract a trio. Times this answer by 1.5. Finally, take away 9.5.

    The skull has _____ bones.

2. How many bones does the human skeleton contain? Do the following math correctly and you'll find out.

    Take a ton and add two centuries to it. Divide 25 times two into the answer. Times this answer by 5 point 5. Now subtract 36 from the answer.

    The human skeleton has _____ bones.

3. Find and circle six bones hiding in the groups of scattered letters. Go from left to right.

tralschy	oidmtar	salrit	paul	nate
brnasa	lowxyg	tmber	vico	ccyx
stern	thorac	risac	rumc	foli

4. Spell the names of four bones from the following letters. You must use 27 of the letters. Place the answers next to each clue.

r	l	n	u	p	c	m	a	s	r
f	u	a	v	l	e	s	c	t	e
e	m	r	u	e	a	i	l	c	a

    Clue: Biggest bone in the body   _ _ _ _ _

    Clue: Known as the breastbone   _ _ _ _ _ _ _

    Clue: Called a shoulder blade   _ _ _ _ _ _ _

    Clue: Referred to as a collarbone   _ _ _ _ _ _ _ _

    Bonus Item: Combine the remaining three letters to form an answer to this statement:

    The smallest bones in the human body are found in the _ _ _.

5. *Bone Riddles*:

    a. What are a golfer's favorite bones?

    b. What is a math teacher's favorite bone?

LS–36
Human Muscle System, Part 1

Let's test your "Muscle I.Q." Use the clues to complete the puzzle.

Across

2. _____ muscles are attached to bones
3. Smooth muscle lines these walls
6. Attaches muscles to bones
9. The shortening of a muscle
10. Muscle you cannot control

Down

1. Muscles always work in _____
4. Heart muscle
5. A muscle that bends a joint
7. Muscle within your control
8. A muscle known to straighten a joint

Muscle Riddle: Ask yourself: "What holds a muscle together?"

LS–37
Human Muscle System, Part 2

1. There are more than 600 muscles in your body. After completing this activity, you'll know at least six of them! Use the clues in the rhymed verse to find each muscle.

   a. I'm not part of a swine,
      but might be cord or twine.   _ _ _ _ t _ _ _ _   muscle

      Another hint: If hope looks dim, try another limb.

   b. Don't look so meek;
      look to the cheek.   _ _ s _ _ t _ _   muscle

      Another hint: Rhymes with ambassador.

   c. Just turn your neck;
      it's there, by heck.   _ t _ _ _ o _ _ s _ _ _ d   muscle

      Another hint: First five letters mean strict;
      letters 7 through 10 produce a support
      for sails on a vessel.

   d. This one makes you feel smart
      because it comes from the heart.   _ _ _ _ _ _ c   muscle

      Another hint: An "a" for spaces two and six.

   e. Flex your arm and study the hump—
      not too heavy? Then start to pump.   _ _ _ e _   muscle

      Another hint: There's "ice" in the middle.

   f. It gives the shoulder strength, shape, and pride,
      and helps raise the arm away from the side.   _ _ _ _ _ i _   muscle

      Another hint: Rhymes with avoid and annoyed.

2. *Tissue Puzzler:* There's a tissue in your body that binds together and supports other tissues and organs. Name it. Here's a hint: tissuetissuetissuetissuetissue—a real connection.

   _ _ n _ e _ _ i _ _   tissue

© 2001 by The Center for Applied Research in Education

LS–38
Human Digestive System

Your digestive system breaks down food into simpler substances as you eat. The process continues for several hours. Some digested materials are absorbed into the bloodstream; the nonabsorbed substances leave the body as waste material.

1. *First-Half Action*: Eight terms related to digestion from the mouth to the stomach lie scattered about. Use the clues to help you put them together. List the completed terms in alphabetical order on the lines under the clues.

   tee   me   cus   ag   bo   ma   oph   chy   ta

   mu   lus   es   us   gla   sto   ch   th   nds   ste

   CLUES: tears and crushes food; produces saliva; ball of chewed food; buds help tongue do this; helps food move through esophagus; tube connecting mouth to stomach; organ for storing food; mixture of food and gastric juice in the stomach

   _____   _____

   _____   _____

   _____   _____

   _____   _____

2. *Last-Half Action*: Draw a line through the eight terms related to digestion from the stomach to the anus. Words may be diagonal, up, or backward.

   ```
   e n i t s e t n i l l a m s
   a s a e r c n a p i s y z e
   x l u n g s f x v p k o i y
   o m u t c e r e q w u l s e
   n s x j c t r l n o l o c p
   a p l e u r a i z i l k n y
   l i s n o t m b v n i a r b
   ```

   List the terms in alphabetical order in the spaces below.

   _____   _____

   _____   _____

   _____   _____

   _____   _____

LS–39
Human Circulatory System

Humans have a closed circulatory system. This means blood moves within vessels that carry it to every part of the body.

1. *Circulatory Terms*: Use the three-word clues to help you identify major terms related to the circulatory system.

Terms	**Clues**
a. _ _ _ _ _ _ _ _ _	blood, heart, away
b. _ _ _ _ _ _ _ _ _	term means vessel
c. _ _ _ _ _ _	upper heart chamber
d. _ _ _ _ _ _ _ _ _ _ _	lower heart chamber
e. _ _ _ _ _ _ _ _ _ _	heart, lungs, flow
f. _ _ _ _ _	largest body artery
g. _ _ _ _ _	blood to heart
h. _ _ _ _ _ _ _ _ _ _ _	arteries, veins, connect
i. _ _ _ _ _	pump, muscle, blood
j. _ _ _ _ _ _	controls blood flow
k. _ _ _ _ _ _	yellowish, blood, water

2. *Destination Lungs*:

a. Blood goes from the right side of the heart to the lungs. Complete the diagram below by filling in the blanks with the structures inside the box.

right atrium	pulmonary artery	veins	lungs
pulmonary artery	branches	right ventricle	

blood → _____ → _____ → _____ →

_____ → _____ → _____

b. Blood enters the lungs, picks up _____ and releases

_____ _____ (2 words).

Fill in the empty spaces with two of these terms.

systemic	aorta	oxygen	platelets	carbon monoxide
carbon dioxide	helium	alveoli	nitrogen	plasma

© 2001 by The Center for Applied Research in Education

(continued)

LS–39 (continued)

3. *Straight from the Heart*: Unscramble the letters in parentheses. Fill in the spaces with the unscrambled terms.

Oxygen-rich blood returns from the lungs and enters the (felt umatir)

_ _ _ _ _ _ _ _ _ _. It continues to the (tfel evelcnirt) _ _ _ _

_ _ _ _ _ _ _ _ _. From there it goes to the (aroat) _ _ _ _ _.

The (rtaao) _ _ _ _ _ branches into (reiersta) _ _ _ _ _ _ _ _ that

carry blood to various parts of the body.

LS–40
Human Respiratory System

Definitions or descriptions for 20 different respiratory terms appear below. Only a part of each term is revealed. Find the missing part for each term and write it in the space provided.

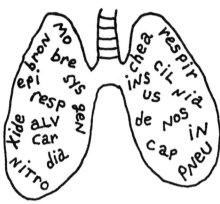

1. Air contains about 78 percent _ _ _ _ _gen.

2. Upper air passages are covered with tiny hairlike structures known as _ _ _ia.

3. The act of inhaling and exhaling air is called _ _ _ _ _ _ation.

4. Openings in the nose are referred to as _ _ _trils.

5. The air you breathe passes the throat and enters the windpipe or tra_ _ _ _ _.

6. Air travels from the windpipe to the _ _ _ _chi.

7. The air eventually reaches the _ _ _eoli sacs where the exchange of oxy_ _ _ and _ _ _bon dio_ _ _ _ takes place.

8. Alveoli is plural for alveol_ _.

9. The _ _ _ _iratory _ _ _tem brings oxygen into the body.

10. The _ _ _glottis is a flap of tissue covering the opening to the trachea.

11. Lungs _ _flate when air pressure decreases in the chest.

12. Lungs _ _flate when air pressure increases in the chest.

13. When you _ _ _athe, air enters and leaves the lungs.

14. A partition of muscle that helps in the breathing process is the _ _ _phragm.

15. The process of taking air into the lungs is known as _ _ _piration.

16. Gas exchange in the lungs takes place between the _ _ _illaries and alveoli.

Bonus Puzzler: Three word fragments NOT USED in the 20 terms fit together to spell the answer to this question: If you develop inflammation of the lungs, what respiratory disease might you have? Answer: _____

106

Name _____   Date _____

LS–41
Human Excretory System

Solid and liquid waste materials are eliminated from the body through the excretory system. Let's take a closer look.

1. *Friendly Filters*:

    a. Kidneys function as the body's filtering organ. They separate water and waste products from the blood and excrete them as _ _ _ _ _ through the _ _ _ _ _ _ _. Use ALL the letters in LEAD, BURN, and DIRE to complete the statement.

    b. The waste liquid contains excess _ _ _ _ _, _ _ _ _ _ _, and other wastes. Liquid wastes leave each kidney through a tube called a _ _ _ _ _ _. The letters needed to fill in the empty spaces are scattered in the sketch below. Use the seven remaining letters to answer the bonus question.

    Bonus Question: What is the name of the tube that carries wastes outside of the body? The tube is called the _ _ _ _ _ _ _.

```
        wa
    sa      ur
    ur  l  et
         et   h
      r    ts
       ra te
         er
```

2. *Skin Is In*: Liquid wastes leave the body through the skin when you perspire. What structures allow this to happen? The letters that spell the name of the structures appear in the puzzle. Which ones are they? HINT: If you want to see the light, start your count from left to right: 12-2-14-15-16 (first word); 22-24-27-29-31-33 (second word).

a	w	p	f	o	n	i	u	n	h	b
s	k	e	a	t	q	l	a	m	d	g
j	l	e	s	a	g	n	v	d	r	s

Answer: _ _ _ _ _   _ _ _ _ _ _ (two words)

107

© 2001 by The Center for Applied Research in Education

LS–42
Human Nervous System

The nervous system keeps you in contact with your environment. It controls and coordinates all the activities of the body. Circle every other letter in the series of letters below. Then unscramble the letters to form a word associated with the nervous system. Write the word on the line above the two clues.

1. kiyawphn

———————————————————————
transmitted sensation

2. jsbexldicmgpku

———————————————————————
nerve message

3. gopritxmbo

———————————————————————
muscles, neuron

4. ateiomtsflmukscu

———————————————————————
produces response

5. akpimson

———————————————————————
sense organ

6. domapntx

———————————————————————
impulses, away

7. ermnoetnvupo

———————————————————————
nerve cell

8. orjdltbncexipemd

———————————————————————
carries impulse

9. afmxcelrdenl

———————————————————————
automatic response

10. matgwasgmnoivl

———————————————————————
nerve clusters

11. fezloucbhlarsckenevm

———————————————————————
maintains balance

12. mptaasxydnisre

———————————————————————
tiny gaps

13. buteyromaclekrwb

———————————————————————
memory, intelligence

14. zeugeionrmqsteyn

———————————————————————
covering membrane

15. aicrxnfbla

———————————————————————
thought center

Bonus Problem: The adult brain weighs about three pounds. Ken, an adult, weighs 162 pounds. What percentage of body weight does his brain represent?

Ken's brain represents _____ percent of his body weight.

LS–43
Human Sensory System

Use the three-word clues in the left column to help you identify the terms associated with the sensory system. Write the term for the clues on the lines. Then unscramble the circled letters in the terms to answer the bonus question.

Three-Word Clues	Term
1. sweet, salty, sour	_ _ _ _ _
2. brain, impulses, waves	_ _ _ Ø _
3. nerve endings, stimuli	_ _ _ _ _ _ _ _ _
4. organ, iris, cornea	_ _ _
5. reaction to stimulation	_ _ _ _ Ø _ _ _ _
6. sense of touch	_ _ _ _ _ _ _
7. nerve, smell, odor	_ _ _ _ _ _ _ _ _
8. activates and excites	_ _ Ø _ _ _ _
9. receptors for taste	_ _ _ _
10. organ, dermis, covering	_ _ _ _
11. blocks sensory nerves	_ _ _ _ Ø _ _ _ _ _
12. organ, food, chemicals	_ _ _ _ _ _
13. a taste sensation	_ _ _ _ _ _
14. neurons carry these	_ _ _ _ _ _ Ø _
15. eye, controls light	_ _ _ _
16. organ, balance, fluids	_ _ Ø
17. smell/taste combined	_ _ _ _ _ _

Bonus Question: What part of the eye contains light-sensitive cells?

Answer: _____

LS–44
Human Endocrine System

Your endocrine system contains glands that produce hormones. These hormones (chemical secretions) control various bodily activities. Too much or too little secretion of hormones from one or more of the endocrine glands may disturb the balance of the body.

1. *Gland Parade*: Use the clues to identify six endocrine glands in the human body.

	Clues
G _ _ _ _	produces reproductive cells
_ _ _ _ _ _ L	produces adrenalin
_ _ A _ _	female sex gland
_ _ N _ _ _	produces melatonin
_ _ _ _ _ _ D	controls metabolism
_ _ _ _ _ S	fights infection

2. *Where Is It?*: Identify the area where each gland below is located by circling one of the body structures listed next to it.

   a. adrenal   lungs, tarsal, liver, brain, kidney
   b. pituitary   heart, brain, stomach, throat, carpal
   c. thyroid   mouth, spine, neck, lungs, leg
   d. pancreas   spine, heart, brain, stomach, genital
   e. teste   pelvic area, male; pelvic area, female

3. *The Right Connection*: Draw a line connecting the endocrine gland, hormone produced, and hormone function in the columns below.

Endocrine Gland	**Hormone**	**Function**
adrenals	insulin	prepares body for stress
pituitary	thyroxin	regulates blood–sugar levels
pancreas	estrogen	controls/regulates female organs
testes	adrenalin	controls growth and other glands
thyroid	testosterone	controls/regulates male organs
ovaries	body growth hormone	controls rate of metabolism

Thought Provoker: What 11-word mode of transportation allows hormones to get around? CLUE: Rhymes with gene and spleen.

Answer: _ _ _ _ _ _ _ _ _ _ _

110

Name _____   Date _____

LS–45
Human Reproductive System

Definitions or descriptions for 25 different human reproductive terms appear below. Only a part of each term is revealed. Find the missing part for each term in the box and write it in the spaces provided.

nis	ovi	men	lar	gene	ovul	duct	am	umb	vag
ovar	centa	tion	ges	zy	strual	co	test	uter	
pla	tes	fall	uter	fe	est	otic	chromo		

1. Eggs and sperm carry __ __ __ __tic information from one generation to the next.
2. The pe__ __ __ is the male organ for reproduction.
3. Se__ __ __ is a mixture of sperm and fluid.
4. The __ __ __ __ __ies produce eggs in the female.
5. After an egg is released, it enters the ovi__ __ __ __.
6. Fertilization usually takes place in an __ __ __duct.
7. The __ __ __ina is known as the birth canal.
8. The men__ __ __ __ __ __ cycle involves egg production and menstruation.
9. Another word for fertilization is concep__ __ __ __.
10. A fertilized egg usually implants in the __ __ __ __us.
11. When fertilization occurs, a __ __gote forms.
12. Each sex cell contains 23 __ __ __ __ __ __somes.
13. The egg is much __ __ __ger than a sperm cell.
14. __ __ __tes produce sperm.
15. The female hormone, __ __ __rogen, starts the maturation of egg cells in the ovaries.
16. The male hormone, __ __ __ __osterone, promotes the growth of facial and body hair in males.
17. Another name for oviduct is __ __ __ __opian tube.
18. The womb is another name for __ __ __ __us.
19. The amni__ __ __ __ sac cushions and protects the developing baby.
20. __ __ __ __ation is the release of an egg from its capsule.
21. The __ __ilical __ __rd connects the embryo to the __ __ __centa.
22. The embryo receives food and oxygen while in the mother through the pla__ __ __ __ __.
23. The later stages of an embryo is known as a __ __tus.
24. Pregnancy is also referred to as the __ __ __tation period.
25. The innermost membrane of the sac enclosing the embryo is called __ __nion.

LS–46
Infectious Diseases

An infectious disease can be spread to others by coughing and sneezing, through food and water contamination, and by contact with an infected person.

Use your creative-thinking ability to find answers to each of the following items:

1. Where would a selfish, greedy person be in a PATHOGEN?

2. Find an electrically charged atom in INFECTION.

3. Where would a single unit be located in the SALMONELLA? (Salmonella bacteria causes food poisoning.)

4. Locate a prefix for "one only" in IMMUNIZATION.

5. Where does everything come to a halt in HISTOPLASMOSIS? (Respiratory disease spread through pigeon waste.)

6. Reveal where a division of drama appears in BACTERIA.

7. Identify a three-letter word meaning life in ANTIBIOTIC.

8. Find a four-letter word in VACCINATION that means "cow" in Latin. HINT: The word rhymes with hack and sack.

9. Find where an offense against any law or code occurs in DISINFECTANT.

10. Where would the prefix for "used before" appear in TRANSMIT?

11. Where does a horse-drawn carriage occur in COMMUNICABLE?

12. Where does decomposition appear in PROTIST?

13. Find a three-letter word for "not" in MONONUCLEOSIS.

14. Reveal a bull-like animal in CHICKEN POX.

15. Where would you find a healing mark on SCARLET FEVER?

Bonus Try: What does this illustration show?

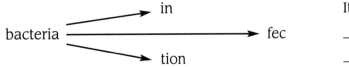

It shows the presence of a

_____ and

_____ infection.

© 2001 by The Center for Applied Research in Education

LS–47
Chronic Disorders

A chronic disorder lasts a long time without any rapid change. It can reoccur at any time. Allergies, kidney disease, cancer, bronchitis, epilepsy, and arthritis are examples of chronic disorders.

1. *Allergy Alert*: Allergens are substances that can cause allergies. A person may have an allergic reaction upon contact with an allergen. Broken words describing allergic reactions appear in the box below. Combine a number from each column to complete the description for each allergic reaction. Begin with Number 1. Write the combined numbers in the spaces under the columns. The first one is done for you.

1.	contin	9.	ging	17.	ing
2.	tick	10.	head	18.	nose
3.	stuf	11.	ly	19.	rash
4.	itch	12.	uous	20.	cough
5.	feel	13.	ing	21.	tired
6.	nag	14.	y	22.	sneezing
7.	pounding	15.	fy	23.	throat
8.	trouble	16.	breath	24.	ache

1, 12, 22; _____; _____; _____;

_____; _____; _____; _____

2. *Chronic Company*: Use the clues to help you fill in the spaces with the letters that spell the names of chronic disorders.

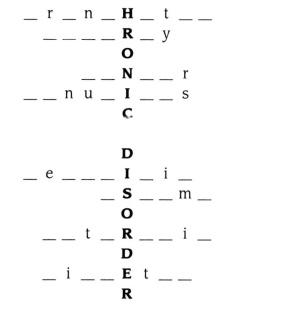

C	**Clues**
_ r _ n _ **H** _ t _ _	inflamed bronchial tubes
_ _ _ _ **R** _ y	reaction to allergens
O	
_ _ **N** _ _ r	uncontrolled cell growth
_ _ n u _ **I** _ _ s	sinus inflammation
C	

D	
_ e _ _ _ **I** _ i _	inflammation of the liver
_ **S** _ _ m _	breathing difficulties
O	
_ _ t _ **R** _ _ i _	inflammation of the joints
D	
_ i _ _ **E** t _ _	created by lack of insulin
R	

LS–48
Use of Drugs

Fill in the spaces with terms related to the use of drugs. Use the clues and letters in the puzzle to assist you.

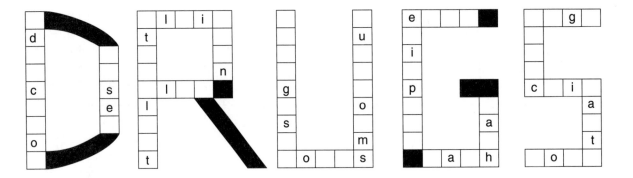

Clues

1. An uncontrollable dependence on a drug.
2. A drug that speeds up the central nervous system.
3. Drug tablets or capsules swallowed whole (appears backward).
4. Some people take narcotics to relieve this.
5. The abbreviation for a hallucinatory drug produced in chemical laboratories.
6. A drug produced to relieve pain.
7. Drinks containing caffeine.
8. Drugs taken at various intervals.
9. Where psilocybin comes from.
10. Comes from the opium poppy (appears from bottom to top).
11. Additional effects brought on by a drug (appears backward).
12. Short for hashish.
13. To perceive sounds while under the influence of a drug (appears backward).
14. Outward symptom of drug use.
15. Groups who practice drug-related rituals (appears from bottom to top).
16. Used to hold a marijuana cigarette.
17. A group assembled for the purpose of taking drugs.
18. The name of the human structure taking drugs.

Name _____ Date _____

LS–49
Use of Alcohol

The following statements regarding the use of alcohol are false. Make each statement true by replacing the underlined word with a term located in the box below. Write the new term on the line.

1. Some people drink to <u>produce</u> feelings of insecurity and inferiority.
   _____

2. Beer contains <u>more</u> alcohol than wine. _____

3. Alcohol is known to <u>regress</u> the nervous system. _____

4. Blood alcohol concentration (BAC) is a measure of the amount of alcohol in the <u>liver.</u> _____

5. Alcohol acts as a depressant. It slows down the actions of the <u>endocrine</u> system.
   _____

6. <u>Rejuvenation</u> may result from alcohol abuse. _____

7. One of the <u>least</u> commonly used drugs is alcohol. _____

8. Alcohol <u>increases</u> the number and intensity of nerve impulses.
   _____

9. <u>Retoxification</u> refers to withdrawal from alcohol. _____

10. Heavy drinking can cause a liver disorder known as <u>halitosis.</u>
    _____

11. <u>Deference</u> is the ability to resist the continued or increasing use of alcohol.
    _____

12. <u>Botulism</u> may result from alcohol abuse. _____

13. Most alcohol is absorbed through the walls of the <u>esophagus</u> and small intestine.
    _____

14. Alcohol causes blood vessels to <u>constrict.</u> _____

15. A <u>distilled</u> beverage results from the breakdown of sugars and starches into alcohol. _____

16. Some people become <u>residually</u> dependent on alcohol. _____

17. <u>Diorite</u> describes a distilled alcoholic drink. _____

18. Large amounts of alcohol slow a person's <u>driving</u> time. _____

19. Alcohol causes the body to <u>gain</u> blood from the capillaries in the skin.
    _____

20. Alcohol is <u>subducted</u> very quickly in the body. _____

physically	less	tolerance	cirrhosis
nervous	liquor	most	alcoholism
metabolized	escape	stomach	fermented
detoxification	reaction	bloodstream	decreases
hallucinations	heat	depress	enlarge

LS–50
Use of Tobacco, Part 1

Use the clues to complete each word associated with the use of tobacco. Then unscramble the circled letters to uncover the answer to the mystery question.

1. A poison found in cigarette tobacco   _ _ s _ n i ◯

2. Virginia Slims™ cigarette ads
    are designed to appeal to this group   _ o _ _ n

3. Known as voicebox   _ a ◯ y _ _

4. Two hundred cigarettes make this   _ _ r _ o _

5. Tiny air sacs in lungs   _ l _ ◯ _ l _

6. Swelling of the bronchi   _ r _ ◯ c _ i _ _ _

7. Lung disability   _ m _ h _ _ e _ _

8. Also known as phlegm   _ _ c _ _ _

9. Body tissue injury   l _ s _ _ ◯

10. Malignant tumor   _ ⓐ _ _ _ _ r

11. Tobacco powder taken by inhaling   _ n _ _ _ _

12. Copenhagen™, for example   ◯ _ e _

13. Expel air suddenly   _ _ u ◯ _

14. Strongest known addition   _ ◯ _ o _ _ n _

15. Dulls senses of taste and smell   _ m ◯ _ _ n _

16. An automatic action; difficult to break   _ _ _ i _

Mystery Question: What do you call any substance that produces cancer?
The substance is known as a _ _ _ _ _ _ _ _ _ _ _.

LS-51
Use of Tobacco, Part 2

1. What structures of the human body are known to suffer damage as a result of tobacco use? Use the letters in DON'T SMOKE to help you identify these structures. The clues will help you find the answers.

	Clues
D _ _ _ _ _	under layer of skin
_ _ _ O _ _	narrow passage in neck
_ _ N _ _ _	organ of speech
_ _ T _ _ _ _ _	blood carriers
_ _ S _ _ _	consists of cells
_ _ M _	flesh inside of mouth
_ _ O _ _ _ _ _ _	food passageway
_ _ _ K _	burning vaporous matter
_ _ _ _ _ E _	known as windpipe

2. Many people find cigarette smoking offensive. They say smokers have _ _ _ _ breath, _ _ _ _ _ _ _ hair, and release secondhand _ _ _ _ _ into the air. Use the scattered letters below to spell the missing words in the paragraph above. RULE: You must use all of the letters.

s		d	s	o	e	l
y	e	m	a	l	k	m	b

3. Write a response to each of the following items:

   a. Marvin began smoking cigarettes at the age of 13. He recently celebrated his 72nd birthday. Marvin says that he's giving up smoking for good. Is it too late for Marvin? Why or why not?

   b. Gloria pays $2.35 a pack for cigarettes. She says she'll quit smoking if the price of cigarettes goes up. Do you believe a rise in price will stop Gloria from smoking? Why or why not?

   c. Mary and Don do not allow smoking in their home. In fact, they post no smoking signs in every room, including the bathrooms. Some guests consider this rude behavior. What do you think?

Name _____   Date _____

LS–52
Heredity, Part 1

Heredity is the passing of traits from the parent to offspring through genes in the chromosomes. Traits are specific characteristics like skin color, eye color, shape of nose, and so on.

A. *Class Act*: Ms. Bunning, science teacher, wanted to find out how many of her students could roll their tongues, an inherited trait. Twelve of her 33 students did it. What percentage of Ms. Bunning's class carried the trait?

_____ percent of students

Do you think the class represents the total human population of tongue rollers? Why or why not?

B. *You Are What You Receive*: The traits you inherit from your parents make up your heredity. Use any SIX of your traits to describe your physical appearance. Underline EACH trait in the description.

C. *Setting Things Straight*: Unscramble the following sentences. Then place the numbers of each sentence on the sketch of the animal cell to show where these structures are located.

1. nucleus activities cellular The controls.

2. heredity Chromosomes cell a in control the nucleus of.

3. are on Genes chromosomes found.

4. traits all the organism Genes of control an.

D. *Just for Fun*: Try this mini-puzzler: If the letters in the word ORGANISM represented different traits, how many traits would an ORGANISM have? It would have _____ traits.

LS–53
Heredity, Part 2

DNA, the basic material of heredity, is found in every cell of the human body. It contains the genetic code and transmits the hereditary pattern. DNA is the substance that determines eye color, hair color, shape of earlobes, and so forth.

A. *Thanks, DNA*: DNA is short for deoxyribonucleic acid. Molecules of DNA make up chromosomes. These molecules contain genes. Why do scientists refer to DNA as the code of life?

B. *Twenty Letters*: Twenty letters spell deoxyribonucleic acid. Use the letters to spell the names of seven body structures—organs or tissues—known to contain DNA. RULE: Identify body structures from the neck up. You may use a letter more than once. The clues will help you find the answers.

Organ/Tissue	Clues
1. _____	gaze, glance
2. _____	tympanum, labyrinth
3. _____	white, gray matter
4. _____	connective tissue, calcium
5. _____	tissue, oxygen
6. _____	protoplasm, unit
7. _____	message, cell

C. *Spiralling DNA*: DNA contains information needed to control cell activities. It also codes and stores information. Scientists say a DNA molecule looks like a twisted ladder with rungs (steps) made of nitrogen bases. Use the information in the preceding sentence to help you sketch a DNA molecule in the box.

D. *Think About It*: A DNA molecule may contain a large number of genes. How could this affect different organisms on Earth?

LS–54
Heredity, Part 3

A. *Genetic Connection*: Genetics is the branch of biology that studies heredity, the passing of traits from parent to offspring. Draw a line through the five words that relate to genetics. Words may be up, backward, or forward.

```
s  s  o  r  c  t
e  h  i  j  u  l
n  a  c  o  d  e
e  t  e  m  a  g
g  t  i  a  r  t
```

List the words below.

_____

_____

B. *Mendel's Magic*: Gregor Mendel is called the Father of Genetics. He did many experiments with pea plants. Draw a line through the traits related to the length of a pea plant and the texture of its pods. Words may be up, backward, or forward.

```
p  s  m  o  o  t  h  w
i  e  t  r  o  h  s  o
l  y  a  l  j  i  t  a
c  k  l  u  t  n  e  b
d  e  l  k  n  i  r  w
```

The four words are: _____

_____

C. *Too Many P's*: Four common genetic terms beginning with the letter p are hidden in the puzzle. Draw a line through each term. Words may be diagonal, backward, or forward.

```
p  u  p  p  k  p  p  p  p  p  y  p  p  o
p  p  p  p  p  p  p  g  p  t  p  p  p  p
h  p  p  e  p  p  p  i  p  j  p  p  p
p  t  p  p  d  p  l  p  z  p  p  i  p
p  a  p  n  y  p  i  s  c  p  p  p  p  p
p  p  p  e  p  b  p  g  p  u  p  p  p  w
p  r  p  p  a  p  p  p  r  p  p  p  p  b
p  d  p  b  p  l  p  e  p  e  p  v  p  p
p  p  o  p  p  p  p  p  p  e  p  p  p
p  r  p  p  x  p  q  p  p  m  p  p  p  p
p  h  e  n  o  t  y  p  e  p  p  f  p  p
```

The four words are: _____

_____

LS–55
Evolution, Part 1

Evolution may be described as the development or change of an organism from its original state to its present state. Replace the capitalized words in each statement below with words that make the statement true. Then rewrite the statement on the lines.

1. Some or all life was *RECENTLY* believed to originate from *LIVING* matter through a process known as spontaneous *REGENERATION.*

   _____
   _____
   _____

2. The processes of evolution occur at a *FAST* pace and are *EASY* to test *NONEXPERIMENTALLY.*

   _____
   _____

3. Charles Darwin's theory included a process of natural *REJECTION.* He favored "the survival of the *FATTEST*" concept.

   _____
   _____

4. Darwin *DIDN'T* believe species change with time. He included his observations in a book titled *THE BIRTH OF MAMMALS,* published in 1859.

   _____
   _____
   _____

5. If an organism's *UNINHERITED* features change over time, we see strong *REVOLUTIONARY* evidence.

   _____
   _____

6. Jean Baptiste de Lamarck, a French scientist, believed that characteristics an organism develops during its life *ARE* passed on to its *PARENTS.*

   _____
   _____
   _____

7. Darwin believed that a *DEVIATION* is an appearance of an inherited trait that makes an individual *SIMILAR TO* other members of the same species.

   _____
   _____
   _____

LS–56
Evolution, Part 2

Evolution refers to change, a process by which organisms change over time.

A. *Land Changes*: The unsettled earth continues to change the face of the land. List four natural events capable of producing land changes.

_____

_____

_____

_____

B. *One Leads to Another*: Organisms, in order to survive, must adjust to environmental changes in the Earth's crust. Use A, D, A, P, and T as the first letters in the names of 10 organisms that have adapted to changing environmental conditions.

A: _____   _____

D: _____   _____

A: _____   _____

P: _____   _____

T: _____   _____

C. Match the term or name with the two-word clue.

Term	**Clue**
a. _ _ a _ _	characteristic, tall
b. _ _ r _ _ t _ _ _ _	organisms, differences
c. p _ _ _ _ a _ _ _ n	group members
d. _ o _ _ i _ s	remains, preserved
e. _ _ n _ h	Darwin, bird
f. g _ _ d _ _ l _ _ _	process, slow
g. _ _ t _ _ c _ _ _ _	death, species
h. L _ m _ _ _ _	acquired characteristics
i. _ a _ w _ _	natural selection
j. B _ _ g _ _	ship, Darwin

D. *Evolution Problem*: Use the following items to illustrate evolution:

time   change   _____

LS-57
Ecology, Part 1

Ecology is the study of the relationship between living things and their environments. The following activity presents eight terms related to ecology.

Round 'Em Up: Circle the word or term hidden in the group of words that matches each statement below.

1. The role of an organism in its environment.

> bioticprecipitategrasslandomnivore
> carnivorenichepredatoroceancyclica

2. Organisms that act upon each other.

> biomeherbivorereactinteractmonkeys
> cheetahslionsalligatorspopulations

3. Total populations of a certain area.

> organellesecosystemnichehabitation
> forestscommunitywaterbiomevertical

4. An organism that makes its own food.

> mineralconsumercarnivoredecompose
> herbivoreproducerscavengeromnivore

5. These return materials from dead organisms to the soil.

> consumerproducerscavengerbiomerole
> abioticsecondarydecomposermammalia

6. An organism that eats other organisms.

> herbivoreconsumersecondarybivalves
> successionalgaeprimaryeatersniches

7. A large area with the same climate and vegetation.

> earthmountainvalleybiomepopulation
> consumerpeakcanyoncratersuccession

8. The area where an organism grows or lives.

> ecosystemprimarybiomebiospherezone
> nichehabitatomnivorelifepopulation

LS–58
Ecology, Part 2

What environmental factors determine the kinds and amount of life found on Earth? Let's find out.

1. *Life Dominates*: Unscramble the four words and use them to fill in the empty spaces.

   Organisms are plentiful in areas with sufficient _ _ _ _ _ _ _ _ _,
   high _ _ _ _ _ _ _ _ _ _ _ _ _, _ _ _ _ _ soil, and _ _ _ _ _ rainfall.

   maple, estemetarpur, hicr, nsehnuis

2. *Soup's On!*: A food chain is the passage of energy and materials through animals and plants in an ecosystem. Show, using arrows, how a food chain might develop in each of the following:

   a. weeds, sun, mouse, owl, snake

      Food chain: _____

   b. large protozoans, small crustaceans, fish, giant water bugs, diatoms, herons

      Food chain: _____

      _____

3. *Finding the Truth*: Circle the letter preceding each true statement below.

   a. Tapeworms are nonparasitic in a food chain.
   b. Grasshoppers are producers in a food chain.
   c. A food web is a series of overlapping food chains.
   d. Deer are considered decomposers in a food web.
   e. Abiotic refers to nonliving matter.
   f. A predator does not play the role of consumer.
   g. Mutualism and commensalism mean the same thing.
   h. Succession in an ecosystem is a rapid process.
   i. The sun is the main source of energy in most ecosystems.
   j. The climax community is the first stage of succession.
   k. The place where an organism lives is its niche.
   l. Predation means the same as parasitism.
   m. All green plants are producers.

Bonus Problem: Unscramble the letters preceding the true statements for the answer to this question: What do you call a "carnivore cuisine"? _____

Part III

Physical Science

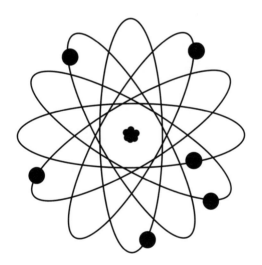

PS–1
Physical Science Puzzle

1. Use the clues to help you identify 21 terms commonly used in the study of physical science.

Clues

_ _ _ **P** _ _ _ _	chemically combined elements
H _ _ _	energy; molecules in motion
_ _ _ _ _ **Y**	produces change in matter
_ _ **S** _	produces hydroxide ions
_ _ _ _ **I** _ _	unite with oxygen
_ _ _ _ _ **C** _ _	change; no new substance
_ _ _ _ **A** _ _ _ _ _	bending of light waves
_ _ **L** _ _ _ _ _	compound; smallest part
_ _ _ **S**	amount of matter
_ _ _ **C** _ _ _ _ _ _ _ _	a lemon cell produces this
_ _ _ _ _ **I** _	energy in motion
_ _ **E** _ _ _ _ _	change; a new substance forms
_ _ _ **N** _	energy; vibrating matter
_ **C** _ _	produces hydrogen atoms
_ _ _ _ **E** _	has weight; occupies space
_ _ _ **P** _ _ _ _ _ _	mixture; large particles
_ _ _ _ _ _ **U** _	prism; colored bands
_ _ _ _ **Z** _	change into ions
Z _ _ _	metal; atomic number 30
_ **L** _ _ _	brass or steel, for example
_ _ _ **E** _	the rate at which work is done

2. *Physical Science Puzzlers*:

    a. There are 50 states in the United States. In how many states would you find MATTER?

    b. Mechanical energy is the total kinetic energy and potential energy in a system. Create a simple way of producing mechanical energy by using a wooden board, hammer, and nail.

PS–2
M and S Terms

1. *Get a Clue*: All of the physical science terms below begin with the letter m or s. Use the clues to help you identify them.

a.	_ _ ○ _ ○ _	has mass; takes up space
b.	_ _ _ _ _ ○	dissolved in a solvent
c.	_ _ ○ _ _	phase of matter
d.	_ _ _ _ _	an object's matter
e.	_ _ ○ _ ○	energy from the sun
f.	_ _ ○ _ _	rate of motion
g.	_ _ ○ _ _	volcanic product
h.	_ _ _ ○○	SI unit of length
i.	_ ○ _ _ _	aluminum, for example
j.	_ _ _ _ _ _ _ _ _ ○	rolled or hammered metal
k.	_ ○ _ _ _ _ _	Na, Ca, Zn, etc.
l.	_ _ _ _ _ _	vibrating energy
m.	_ _ _ _ _ _ _ _ _	capable of being mixed
n.	○ _ _ _ _	prefix meaning 1/1000
o.	_ _ ○ _ _ _ _	marsh gas
p.	○ _ _ _ _	compound, NaCL
q.	_ _ ○ _ _ _	SiO$_2$
r.	_ _ _ _ _ ○ _ _	product of mass and velocity
s.	_ _ ○ _ _ ○ _	fixed pulley, for example
t.	_ _ _ _ ○ _ _ _ ○ _	fine solid dispersed in a liquid

2. *These Three Are E's*: The letters needed to spell each answer below are circled in "Get a Clue."

   a. What do you call compounds that conduct electric currents when dissolved or melted? They are known as _ _ _ _ _ _ _ _ _ _ _ _ _.

   b. What term describes matter containing the same atoms? Matter in which all the atoms are alike is an _ _ _ _ _ _ _.

   c. What three-letter word represents a unit of work in the metric system? It is an _ _ _.

PS–3
Physical Scientists

A scientist is a professional person who investigates nature. He or she gathers information, puts it in order, and then uses it to solve a problem or two. A physical scientist studies matter and energy.

A. *Who Did What?*: Column A lists the names of eight scientists. Column B gives the contributions made by the scientists. Write the correct letter from Column B next to the corresponding number in Column A. Use the hints in parentheses to guide you.

Column A	Column B
_____ 1. Dmitri Mendeleyev	a. Discovered polonium and radium (*Last letters 3, 4, and 5 are the same*)
_____ 2. Dorothy Hodgkin	b. Studies the forces that exist within atoms (*An informal greeting appears twice*)
_____ 3. Svante Arrhenius	c. Studied planetary movement (*A girl appears in the first name*)
_____ 4. Wilhelm Roentgen	d. Development of the Periodic Table (*Letters 2, 3, and 4 mean "cease to exist"*)
_____ 5. Marie Curie	e. Laws of Motion (*A salamander is part of name*)
_____ 6. Isaac Newton	f. Molecular structure research (*Has the Spanish name for "gold" in name*)
_____ 7. Chien-Shiung Wu	g. Discoverer of X-rays (*"Fish eggs" in name*)
_____ 8. Johannes Kepler	h. Theory of Ionization (*An animal appears in first and last names*)

B. *Let's Play Scientist*: Examine the items in the box. Use your creative powers to identify the object they represent. Then write a brief statement in support of your answer.

Object: _____

Statement: _____

_____

_____

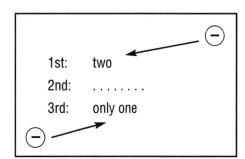

PS–4
Problem Solving

Everyone, including scientists, deals with problems on an ongoing basis. Tough problems produce anxiety in many people, and an anxious person becomes frustrated when a problem leads to a dead-end.

Here's an opportunity to solve eight problems in a playful manner. You'll need to use your ability to think in a creative way. Remember, there's more than one way to solve a problem. Write answers to each problem on the line.

1. What recent decade is represented by these letters:

   d   d   d   d   d   d   d

   _____

2. How many of the following items are lines?

   engineer   cord   ++++++++++   l   path   plumber

   _____

3. How many "eights" can you find below?

   〓 I ∧ I I   ∞   "ates"   8   ⅊

   _____

4. Create *three* animals with the letters a and n in their names from these letters:

   s   i   a   l   a   m   n.   You can use a letter more than once.

   _____

5. Create a way to show that 10 lines equal eight.

   (I I I I I I I I I I = eight)

   _____

6. How many **L**'s are there in one rectangle?

   _____

7. Show how the following cycle occurs thousands of miles from Earth: solid→phase change→solid→phase change.

   _____

8. Use a regular pencil to demonstrate how friction eliminates friction.

   _____

© 2001 by The Center for Applied Research in Education

PS-5
Scientific Laws

Scientific Laws describe a pattern in nature. Certain events occur over and over again. These patterns allow observers to predict the behavior of things.

    Identify the eight scientific laws below by filling in the blanks with the appropriate letters. (The first and last letters of the law have been provided.) Then transfer the numbered letters to the spaces at the bottom of the page. These letters will spell out an important message.

1. Matter cannot be created or destroyed by ordinary chemical means.

    Law of C__ __ __ __ __ __ __ __ __ __N   of   M__ __ __ __R
                                12

2. Every compound always has the same proportion by weight of the elements composing it.

    Law of D__ __ __ __ __ __E   P__ __ __ __ __ __ __ __ __S
                   4   1

3. Every mass in the universe exerts a force of attraction on every other mass.

    Law of U__ __ __ __ __ __ __L   G__ __ __ __ __ __ __ __ __N
                   2

4. Energy cannot be created nor destroyed, but it can change from one form to another.

    Law of C__ __ __ __ __ __ __ __ __ __ N   of   E__ __ __ __Y
                9

5. Pressure applied to a confined liquid acts equally in all directions.

    P__ __ __ __ __'S Law
         5

6. For any confined gas, the pressure multiplied by its corresponding volume is a constant, providing the temperature remains unchanged.

    B__ __ __ __'S Law
       11 8

7. The total momentum of a group of objects does not change unless outside forces act on the objects.

    Law of C__ __ __ __ __ __ __ __ __ __N of M__ __ __ __ __ __M
                 7   3   10

8. An object will not change its motion unless an unbalanced force acts on it.

    Newton's F__ __ __T Law of M__ __ __ __N
           13   6

MESSAGE: A scientific law will __ __ __ __d__ __ __the __ __ __ __ __ __ __ __
                              1 2 3 4 5 6   7 8 9 10 11 12 13

of a given situation.

PS–6
Measurement

1. Ancients used a cubit to measure length. A cubit was the distance on an extended arm and hand from the elbow to the tip of the middle finger. How many cubits are there in EACH of the following objects? Use 17.5 inches for one cubit.

    _____ a. a 16-foot boat   _____ c. a 21-foot Great White Shark

    _____ b. a football field (100 yards)   _____ d. a 46-foot giant squid

2. The metric system is a decimal system of weights and measures. Here are examples of how it compares with the English system:

2.54 centimeters = 1 inch	1 liter = 1.06 quart
100 centimeters = 1 meter	454 grams = 1 pound
1 meter = 39.37 inches	1 kilogram = 2.2 pounds

    Use this information to solve these problems:

    a.   You weigh 134.5 pounds. What is your weight in grams? kilograms?

    b.   You have a 30-inch waist. What is your waist size in centimeters?

    c.   Your volleyball team drank 1,935 quarts of water during the season. How many liters did the team drink?

    d.   You catch a 3.7-pound bass. How many grams does it weigh?

    e.   Christina weighs 59 kilograms. Her friend, Sarah, weighs 6,129 grams. Which girl weighs more?

3. Match each item in the left column with the best response in the right column.

    ____ a. mass   1. force of gravity on an object

    ____ b. millimeter   2. a unit of mass

    ____ c. volume   3. measures distance

    ____ d. weight   4. amount of space matter takes up

    ____ e. gram   5. amount of matter

4. *Bonus Puzzler:* In five words or less, answer these weird questions:

    a.   How long is a piece of thread?

    b.   How high is up?

PS–7
Metric System

Many people in the world, including scientists, use the metric system for measuring length, mass, weight, and volume.

1. *Letter Getter*: Use the clues and the letters from the boxed sentence below to help you identify terms related to the metric system. Place letters in the spaces. You may use a letter more than once. One answer appears three times in the puzzle.

> The CUBIT is an early known measurement of length.

a. 1/100 meter — — — — —

b. mass unit — — — —

c. unit of volume — — — — —

d. 100 cm or 1,000 cm — — — — —

e. equals 100,000 cm — — — — — — — — —

f. 1,000 in a meter — — — — — — — — — — —

g. one cubic centimeter — — — — — — — — — — —

h. equals 2.2 pounds — — — — — — — —

i. prefix for 1/1000 — — — — —

j. basic unit of length — — — — —

k. prefix for 1,000 — — — —

l. volume measurement — — — — —

m. 1/100 of a gram — — — — — — — — —

n. unit of force — — — — — —

o. one inch = 2.54 — — — — — — — — — — — —

p. 39.37 inches — — — — —

2. *Metric Unit Riddle*: What does it take to keep mm's and cm's in line?

_____

3. *Metric Unit Puzzler*: How can you combine a meter and liter to create 5,280 feet? HINT: 5,280 feet equal one mile.

_____

PS–8
A Look at Alchemy

Alchemy, an early form of chemistry, flourished in the Middle Ages. The aim of an alchemist was to turn base metals into gold and to find the "elixir of life"—the secret of eternal youth.

1. *Alchemy "Losers"*: Some alchemists were serious about their work; others chose the "easy, get rich quick" way. Unfortunately, the families of the greedy ones ran out of food and suffered a poverty-stricken existence.

   A foolish person today might wind up like the greedy alchemist: poor, hungry, and frustrated. Briefly describe TWO situations TODAY that could lead to this.

   _____

   _____

   _____

   _____

   _____

2. *Oh to Be Young Again*: A dedicated alchemist searched for the magic formula of youth and ways to perfect humans. Briefly describe FOUR ways some people attempt to preserve their youth.

   _____

   _____

   _____

   _____

   _____

3. *Tools of the Trade*: The labs of alchemists included such items as crucibles, tongs, flasks, mortars and pestles, pots, pans, drug jars, water, animals, toads, vegetables, and minerals. Use your imagination and miscellaneous matter to create a recipe for a perfect medicine or "elixir of life."

   _____

   _____

   _____

   _____

   _____

   _____

PS–9
Introducing Matter, Part 1

Matter is anything that takes up space and has mass. Examples are rocks, coins, air, and people.

1. *Matter from Matter*: Use the letters in MATTER to write the names of 8 examples of matter. You may use a letter more than once.

    _____

    _____

2. *Weight for the Mass*: Mass is the amount of matter. Gravity gives matter weight and weight can be measured with a scale or balance. The amount of matter an object contains remains the same. However, the weight may vary from place to place. For example, if you weigh 120 pounds on Earth, you'll weigh only 20 pounds on the moon. Why? Because the moon has one-sixth the gravitational attraction as that of Earth. Calculate how much each of the following objects would weigh on the moon.

    a.   500 grams of lead   _____ grams (gm)

    b.   23-pound salmon   _____ pounds (lb)

    c.   498-pound rock   _____ pounds (lb)

    d.   528 kilograms of string   _____ kilograms (kg)

    e.   What do you notice about the answers to these four items?

    _____

3. *Matter of Opinion*: Two pieces or parts of matter cannot occupy the same place at the same time. For example, when a ship sinks, it displaces enough water to make room for the ship.

    a.   If you think creatively, you might be able to show how the parts of matter CAN occupy the same place at the same time. Use the space below to complete the task. CAUTION: Expect a trick!

    ┌─────────────────────────────────────┐
    │   ───   │
    └─────────────────────────────────────┘

    b.   How can you produce matter from these numbers and letters?
         one + e + (10+3) + twenty + (9+9) + t

    _____

4. *Radical Riddle:* What do you call matter that suddenly disappears?

PS–10
Introducing Matter, Part 2

Use the clues to help you identify 25 terms related to MATTER.

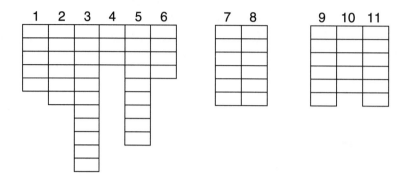

CLUES:

1. iron, for example
2. any base
3. measurement of heat
4. symbol: Sn
5. liquid into vapor
6. oxidized iron
7. needed for combustion
8. melting together
9. no definite shape

10. a mixture of metals
11. force of gravity
12. FeO, for example
13. hydrocarbon
14. neutral atomic particle
15. dissolves solute
16. solar and nuclear, for example
17. Na+Cl yields salt

18. sticky fluid consistency
19. element, smallest particle
20. related to heat
21. electrically charged atom
22. mined minerals
23. four-fifths of atmosphere
24. unites with oxygen
25. a splitting apart

Bonus Challenge: Rearrange the top lines of the five puzzle parts for the answer to the following question:

What law states that matter cannot be created or destroyed by ordinary chemical means?

Answer: ＿ ＿ ＿ ＿   ＿ ＿ ＿ ＿ ＿ ＿ ＿ ＿ ＿ ＿   ＿ ＿

＿ ＿ ＿ ＿ ＿ ＿

PS-11
Matter Puzzlers

1. This box of Brand X cereal measures 11 inches × 2 inches. It weighs 20 ounces. The box of cereal is an example of MATTER because it has _ _ _ _ _ _ and takes up _ _ _ _ _. Describe how to convert the following symbols into the words needed to fill in the empty spaces.

p   [A ♥]   8
w   s

2. Matter exists in three different states of phases: gas, liquid, or solid. Use the two-word clues to help you identify the 10 examples of matter.

		Clues
a.	_ _ _	nitrogen, oxygen
b.	_ _ _ _	class Aves
c.	_ _ _ _ _	metal, round
d.	_ _ _ _ _ _ _ _	draws circles
e.	_ _ _ _ _ _	photosynthesis, green
f.	_ _ _ _ _ _ _ _ _	lightest gas
g.	_ _ _ _ _ _ _ _	Egyptian tomb
h.	_ _ _ _ _ _	hydrogen, oxygen
i.	_ _ _ _ _ _ _	gas, balloons
j.	_ _ _ _ _ _	vaporized water

3. An element is the simplest type of matter. It consists of only one kind of matter. The periodic table of elements lists over 100 elements. Circle the elements in the box below.

water	iron	bronze	zinc	tin	wax	glass
No	brass	cork	salt	K	gb	potassium
Fe	silt	lead	Pb	ink	At	silicon

4. Find and circle five examples of MIXTURES in the following paragraph:

Sonja created a fancy salad for Tony's birthday dinner. She served food on the concrete patio. Clumsy Tony spilled his plate of fried chicken and succotash on the soil under his chair.

5. *Bonus Challenge:* Spell COMPOUND with five letters.

PS–12
State of Matter: Solid

A solid is matter that takes up a definite amount of space and has a definite shape. In short, its shape and volume remain the same.

A. *Solid Stuff*: Fill in the missing letters to complete the terms related to solids. Use the clues to help you find the answers.

Clues

_ _ _ **S** _	1. a way or state
_ **O** _ _	2. xylem material
_ **L** _ _ _ _ _	3. credit card material
_ _ **I** _ _	4. clay; broken or fired
_ _ _ **D** _ _ _ _ _ _	5. heat through solids
_ _ **S** _	6. quantity of matter
_ _ _ _ _ _ **T** _	7. trait or quality
_ _ **A** _ _	8. amorphous solid
_ _ _ _ _ **T** _	9. a solid's thickness
_ _ _ **E** _ _ _ _ _	10. vibrate in place
_ **O** _ _	11. mixture of minerals
F _ _ _ _ _ _ _	12. point; liquid to solid
_ _ _ _ **M** _	13. occupied space
_ _ **A** _ _	14. remains unchanged
_ _ _ **T** _ _ _ _ _	15. these stay together
_ _ _ _ **T** _ _ _	16. geometric patterns
_ _ **E**	17. a solid that melts
_ _ _ _ _ **R**	18. metallic element; Cu

B. *A Couple of Solid Puzzlers*:

Puzzler #1: What part of a solid is REALLY gas?

_____

Puzzler #2: What part of a solid is REALLY solid?

_____

PS–13
State of Matter: Liquid

Liquid is a state of matter having a constant volume but no definite shape. An example is water in its liquid form.

A. *Liquid Crossword Puzzle*: Complete the puzzle using terms or examples related to the liquid state of matter. First fill in the blanks in the words below the puzzle, and you'll have the answers to the puzzle.

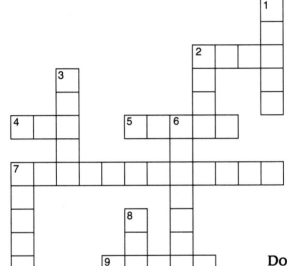

Across

2. _ o _ p
4. _ _ a
5. s _ _ a _
7. c _ n _ _ n _ _ t _ _ n
9. s w _ _ _
10. _ i _ k

Down

1. v _ p _ _
2. _ o _ a
3. _ a _ n
6. _ v _ p _ r a _ _ _ n
7. _ o _ _ e _
8. _ e _

B. *Term Match*: Use the single word clue to identify six terms from Part A.

1. _____   a. food
2. _____   b. perspire
3. _____   c. moo
4. _____   d. pop
5. _____   e. vanish
6. _____   f. shrub

PS–14
State of Matter: Gas

A gas has neither a definite shape nor a definite volume. Oxygen is a good example of a gas.

A. *15 Terms*: Use the clues to help you locate 15 words related in some way to gas. Write the word on the line next to its clue. The first letter of each word is given.

1. Makes up nearly four-fifths of the atmosphere   N_____

2. Takes the shape of this   C_____

3. There's nothing definite here   V_____

4. A rare gas; name means "lazy"   A_____

5. The lightest of all elements   H_____

6. A gas produced from the decomposition of vegetable matter   O_____

7. These are much less in gases than solids or liquids   D_____

8. These move about freely   M_____

9. Gas; heavier than air; doesn't support combustion (2 words)   C_____ D_____

10. Gases that surround us   A_____

11. Discovered oxygen; name rhymes with "beastley"   P_____

12. Used to fill balloons   H_____

13. Combustible gas produced in nature from the decomposition of vegetable matter   N_____

14. Volume of gas depends on two things: pressure and ?   T_____

15. Carbonated beverage fizz; the escape of gas is called ?   E_____

B. *Gas Puzzlers*:

Gas Puzzler #1: Use the FIRST letters in 15, 5, 1, 10, 15, 14 in Part A to identify the following hydrocarbon gas: _ _ _ _ _ _

Gas Puzzler #2: Use the FIRST letters in 14, 10, 15, 1, 8, 5, 15 in Part A to identify another hydrocarbon gas: _ _ _ _ _ _ _

PS-15
Crystal Matter

Crystals are the flowers of the mineral world. These solid substances have a definite shape depending on how their internal atoms are arranged. These atoms form various geometric patterns.

1. *Crystal Line Up*: Let's see how many common crystals you can identify from the two-line verse clues.

   a. Sodium. Saline. What's in a name?
      I come to the table just the same.

      _ _ _ _ crystal

   b. Purple. Violet. A six-sided frame.
      Think about quartz . . . now do you know my name?

      _ _ _ _ _ _ _ _ _ crystal

   c. Iron sulfide keeps me bold
      and the nickname of "fool's gold."

      _ _ _ _ _ _ _ crystal

   d. This is synthetic, sugary and sweet;
      So savor the flavor, enjoy your treat.

      _ _ _ _   _ _ _ _ _ crystal

2. *All but One*: Use all the letters in parentheses (except one) to fill in the blanks.

   a. A crystal's atoms are arranged in definite

      _ _ _ _ _ _ _ _ _ (t s a r p e n d t).

   b. Non-crystalline minerals are known as

      _ _ _ _ _ _ _ _ _ _ (o r m h u s i a o p).

   c. The _ _ _ _ _ _ (b u c i x c) system is the simplest crystal arrangement.

   d. A _ _ _ _ _ _ _ _ _ _ _ (x l a c g h n a o e) crystal has six sides.

   e. Crystals form flat surfaces and straight _ _ _ _ _ _ (s g e d e s).

3. *Bonus Puzzler:* Use the extra letters from b, c, and e above to produce the answer to this question:

   In how many basic systems do minerals crystallize?

   Answer: _____

PS–16
Periodic Table of Elements

A. Complete each item related to the periodic table of elements by writing the word fragments in the right-hand column in the appropriate spaces next to the incomplete term in the left-hand column. Use the hints in parentheses to help you complete each term. (The first one is done for you.) You may want to refer to a periodic table of elements.

1.	lith	_____ium_____	(metal)	con
2.	Berk	_____	(Actinide)	muth
3.	pro	_____	(positive)	ron
4.	hy	_____	(1 electron)	icium
5.	B	_____	(symbol)	ells
6.	sil	_____	(neutrons, 108)	rine
7.	fam	_____	(column)	ver
8.	Bis	_____	(element)	ine
9.	Haf	_____	(solid)	inum
10.	neu	_____	(no charge)	nium
11.	chlo	_____	(gas)	drogen
12.	sili	_____	(metalloid)	ton
13.	elect	_____	(negative)	elium
14.	fluor	_____	(nonmetal)	ium
15.	sh	_____	(k, l, m, etc.)	ily
16.	Plat	_____	(protons, 78)	non
17.	Xe	_____	(noble)	tron
18.	Amer	_____	(artificial)	a

B. *Periodic Table Riddles*:

1. Why is it good to receive things from a neutron?

2. Why did Helen Helium marry Kelly Krypton?

C. *Periodic Table Puzzlers*: Create a way to . . .

- produce a relative by combining Indium with Potassium.

- produce a horse by combining Silver with Nitrogen.

- produce physical suffering by combining Protactinium with Indium.

- produce a bivalve mollusk by combining Americium with Chlorine.

PS-17

Atoms

An atom is the smallest particle of an element—the tiniest piece of any matter. There are sulfur atoms, aluminum atoms, oxygen atoms, and so on.

1. John Dalton, scientist, published his Atomic Theory in 1808. He stated all atoms of iron are exactly alike. All atoms of oxygen are exactly alike, etc. But atoms of iron are different from atoms of oxygen, carbon, and so on. TRY THIS: Use a pencil to write IRON, OXYGEN, and CARBON on a piece of paper. Look closely at each word. Each one represents a different element. What atoms make up each of these elements? HINT: Be a creative thinker.

2. A molecule of water has three atoms: H_2O—2 hydrogen and 1 oxygen. Circle EACH element in the box needed to complete the following compounds:

   methane (gas)—CH_4 calcium chloride—$CaCl_2$
   carbon dioxide—CO_2 calcium sulfate—$CaSO_4$
   silicon dioxide—SIO_2 potassium chloride—KCl
   sulfuric acid—H_2SO_4

O	O	H	H	C	Cl	O	H	O	O	Cl
O	H	Ca	O	Cl	C	O	Si	O	Ca	O
Na	H	O	Cl	S	O	K	H	Ca	S	O

   Two of the uncircled elements combine to form a well-known seasoning.
   What is it? _____

3. Complete each statement with six of the ten words listed in alphabetical order.

   a. Atoms are the basic building block of _____.

   b. The _____ is in the center of an atom.

   c. _____ are negatively charged particles.

   d. A _____ carries a positive charge.

   e. A _____ is a particle believed to make up protons and neutrons.

   f. Most of an atom is empty _____.

   alloy   neutrino
   colloid   nucleus
   electrons   proton
   matter   quark
   metalloid   space

PS–18
Elements Everywhere

1. *Keep It Together*: Fill in the missing letters to complete the definition of an element.

   An element is m_tte_ or su_stan_e that _ann_t be se_ar_te_ into a

   $\underset{1}{\ }\ \underset{2}{\ }$ ... $\underset{3}{\ }\ \underset{4}{\ }$ ... $\underset{5}{\ }\ \underset{6}{\ }$ ... $\underset{7}{\ }\ \underset{8}{\ }\ \underset{9}{\ }$

   s_m_lar s_bs_a_ce. All atoms of an element are the same.
   $\underset{10}{\ }\ \underset{11}{\ }$ ... $\underset{12}{\ }\ \underset{13}{\ }\ \underset{14}{\ }$

   a. Unscramble the letters for spaces 2, 10, 6, and 14
       to spell the name of a common element.   __ __ __ __

   b. Unscramble the letters for spaces 11, 14, and 13
       to spell the name of another common element.   __ __ __

2. *Most "Sootable"*: Use the clues in the following verse and the numbers from the letters in Part 1 above to identify the mystery element.

   > What would nature's diamond be without me?
   > Or numbers 5, 6, 8, 2, 14, and 3?
   > The symbol C will take its toll
   > As pencil lead, coke, and charcoal.

   The mystery element is __ __ __ __ __ __ .

3. *Symbol Soup*: The chemical symbols for six elements are scattered about. Use the paired clues to help you find the chemical symbols.

	e		H		A		I		N	
Z		A		t		g		u		n

Paired Clues		Chemical Symbols
a.	nonmetallic, antiseptic	__
b.	radioactive, bismuth	__ __
c.	heavy, yellow	__ __
d.	gas, inert	__ __
e.	thermometer, liquid	__ __
f.	metal, thirty	__ __

4. *Material Riddle:* Where do children FIRST learn about matter?

PS–19
Chemical Symbols

Chemical symbols are a chemist's shorthand for writing the names of elements. Chemists use one or two letters to identify an element: for example, P for Phosphorus and Mn for Manganese. Here are two rules for writing chemical symbols: (1) The first letter is ALWAYS capitalized. (2) If the symbol is two letters, the second letter is set in lower case.

1. *Chemical Symbol Roundup*: Use the scattered letters below to assign chemical symbols to the elements located under the box. Write the chemical symbol in the space next to the element.

H	g	h	K	b	c	V	a	P	e	A	s	i	S	F	i	S
s	b	a	L	A	t	Y	e	S	t	g	n	R	m	c	u	l

___ a. Ruthenium   ___ g. Selinium

___ b. Fluorine   ___ h. Yttrium

___ c. Vanadium   ___ i. Actinium

___ d. Antimony   ___ j. Silver

___ e. Lead   ___ k. Potassium

___ f. Mercury   ___ l. Sulfur

2. *Extra Letters*: Write the letters you DIDN'T USE from Part 1 on the line below.

_____

Now combine these letters to form answers to the following questions:

a. What group of early experimenters used symbols to identify certain elements?

_ _ _ _ _ _ _ _ _ _

b. From what names do some chemical symbols come from? _ _ _ _ _
names

3. *Keep It Symbol*: Give brief answers to the following questions:

a. Could the initials in your name become chemical symbols?

_____

_____

b. How many atoms are represented in the chemical symbol Sr?

_____

PS–20
Eight Mystery Elements

An element is a substance that cannot be broken down into simpler substances by ordinary means. Let's investigate further.

A. *The Great Eight*: Four clues to the identity of a mystery element are located under the box. Use these hints to reveal the names of eight mystery elements. Write the chemical symbol of the element inside the box.

1. [ ]
- abundant in Earth's crust
- forms lime
- essential to diet
- "hard water" ingredient

2. [ ]
- used in plating
- hard, durable
- silver-white metal
- strong alloy

3. [ ]
- found in living organisms
- graphite and diamond
- good absorbent
- organic chemistry

4. [ ]
- rare earth element
- used in alloys
- named after Ceres
- rhymes with delirium

5. [ ]
- gas
- makes up 78 percent of air
- doesn't support combustion
- colorless, tasteless, odorless

6. [ ]
- ore: galena
- soft, bluish-white
- known to be poisonous
- used in batteries

7. [ ]
- nonmetal
- ancient element
- medicinal use
- yellow solid

8. [ ]
- extremely active
- found in matches
- fertilizer ingredient
- glows in the dark

B. *Element Puzzler:* Use the letters in ELEMENT to write the chemical symbols for six different elements. You may capitalize letters and use a letter more than once. Write the name of the element in parentheses.

____ (_____)   ____ (_____)   ____ (_____)

____ (_____)   ____ (_____)   ____ (_____)

PS–21
Element Rhymers

Use a periodic table to help you find elements that rhyme with the following words. Write the sound-alike elements and their chemical symbols in the appropriate columns. RULE: The element must be BETWEEN the listed atomic numbers.

		Element	Chemical Symbol	Atomic Numbers
1.	moron	_____	_____	1–9
2.	freon	_____	_____	6–11
3.	stink	_____	_____	20–32
4.	swine	_____	_____	40–75
5.	fault	_____	_____	20–40
6.	whopper	_____	_____	22–38
7.	instead	_____	_____	51–87
8.	extreme	_____	_____	5–30
9.	keen	_____	_____	30–42
10.	magazine	_____	_____	70–88
11.	untold	_____	_____	63–85
12.	dumb	_____	_____	25–45
13.	tickle	_____	_____	20–32
14.	cease	_____	_____	15–29
15.	skin	_____	_____	26–30
16.	lunatic	_____	_____	29–39
17.	polygon	_____	_____	32–41
18.	spur	_____	_____	3–24
19.	bony	_____	_____	39–56
20.	bus	_____	_____	2–22

PS–22
Hydrogen

Hydrogen, the lightest element, makes up more compounds than any other element. Hydrogen is a colorless, odorless, and tasteless gas. It appears as number one in the periodic table of elements.

A. *Hydrogen Hotline*: The answers needed to fill the spaces in the statements below are broken and scattered throughout the diagram. Complete the statements by putting the word fragments together.

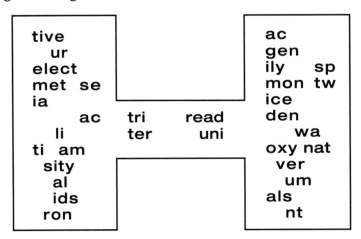

1. Hydrogen is found in all _ _ _ _ _.
2. Hydrogen is not _ _ _ _ _ _ _ at ordinary temperatures.
3. Hydrogen and _ _ _ _ _ _ _ combine to form water.
4. Coal, oil, and _ _ _ _ _ _ _ _ gas contain hydrogen.
5. _ _ _ _ _ _ _ _ is an isotope of hydrogen.
6. Some _ _ _ _ _ _ _ react with acids to form hydrogen.
7. A burning _ _ _ _ _ _ _ is used to test for hydrogen.
8. Hydrogen has one _ _ _ _ _ _ _ _ _ in its only shell.
9. Hydrogen has the lowest _ _ _ _ _ _ _ _ of all elements.
10. Hydrogen burns _ _ _ _ _ _ _ or explodes.
11. Hydrogen is used to make _ _ _ _ _ _ _ _ (NH_3).
12. There is _ _ _ _ _ as much hydrogen in water as oxygen.
13. Hydrogen gas burns in air to form _ _ _ _ _ _.
14. Ninety percent of all the atoms in the _ _ _ _ _ _ _ _ _ are hydrogen.

B. *Hydrogen Riddle:* Why is hydrogen gas not considered a "trendsetter"?

Name _____   Date _____

PS-23
Oxygen

Oxygen is the most abundant element in the Earth's crust. It is a colorless, odorless, tasteless gas that makes up about one-fifth of the atmosphere.

1. *Three Cheers for Oxygen*: Use the clues to help you fill in the empty spaces. ALL answers are related in some way to oxygen.

_ **O** _ _ _	Crustal oxygen containers
_ _ _ **X** _ _ _ _	CO_2: carbon _____
_ _ _ _ _ _ _ _ _ **Y**	Co-discoverer of oxygen
_ _ _ **G** _ _	Atomic number of oxygen
_ _ _ **E** _	Can't exist without oxygen
_ _ _ _ _ _ _ _ **N** _	Oxygen has eight of these
O _ _ _ _ _ _	Compounds of oxygen
_ _ _ _ **X** _ _ _	CO; carbon _____
_ **Y** _ _ _ _	O (element)
_ _ _ _ **G** _	Oxygen involved with this
_ _ _ **E**	Oxygen supports this
_ _ _ _ _ _ **N** _	Oxygen has eight of these
O _ _ _ _ _	An allotrope of oxygen
_ _ **X** _ _ _ _ _	Oxygen part of "jumble"
_ _ _ _ _ _ **Y** _ _ _ _ _ _ _	Oxygen involved here too!
_ _ _ _ _ **G** _ _	Oxygen's water partner
_ _ _ **E** _ _ _ _	Two O_2 atoms; diatomic
_ _ _ **N** _ _ _	Can't continue without O_2

2. *Oxygen Puzzler*: Use the letters in the words below to produce the names of organisms or parts of organisms that need oxygen to remain alive. You may use a letter more than once. Write the names on the line.

    elements: _____

    compounds: _____

    chemistry: _____

    reaction: _____

PS-24
Carbon

1. *Carbon Call*: Circle the letter preceding each TRUE statement regarding carbon.

    a. Carbon atoms do not bond with hydrogen atoms.

    b. Carbon-14, a radioactive isotope, has a half-life of 5,720 years.

    c. Carbon has an atomic number of six.

    d. Carbon combines with sodium to form salt.

    e. Carbon atoms combine readily with other atoms.

    f. Carbon exists in all living things.

    g. The carbon atom has six protons.

    h. Carbon is found in large abundance.

    i. The carbon atom has 4 atoms in its outer energy level.

    j. Gasoline, perfume, and candles contain carbon atoms.

    k. Hydrocarbons form when carbon combines with hydrogen.

    l. Carbon atoms are found in some organic compounds and all inorganic compounds.

    m. Fruit sugar is an example of a carbon compound.

    n. Two crystalline forms of carbon are graphite and diamond.

    o. More than 90 percent of all known compounds contain carbon.

    p. Carbon is classified as a reactive metal.

    q. Carbon seldom combines with oxygen to form compounds.

    r. Carbon atoms can join other atoms in single, double, or triple covalent bonds.

2. *True Carbon*: Count the number of true statements in Part 1 above. The correct number of true statements will provide the answer to this question: What is the atomic mass number of carbon? (circle one)

    a. 8   b. 10   c. 12   d. 14   e. 16

3. *Carbonaceous Cuisine*: Carbonaceous means consisting of or containing carbon. Coal contains carbon; thus, coal is a carbonaceous substance. Use the letters in CARBONACEOUS to write the names of the following carbon-containing items. You may use a letter more than once.

    a. 206 of these in your body   _____

    b. mode of transportation   _____

    c. sweet, curved yellowish fruit   _____

    d. perceives sound   _____

    e. a furry, short-tailed mammal   _____

PS–25
Hydrocarbons

Carbon and hydrogen combine to form hydrocarbon compounds that make up crude oil. For example, CH_4, methane gas, is a hydrocarbon—one carbon atom combined with four hydrogen atoms. Gasoline comes from petroleum. Petroleum is a mixture of hydrocarbons. Methane gas

1. *Puzzling Hydrocarbons*: Two of the five hydrocarbon formulas listed below appear in the puzzle. When you find them, circle the names of the formulas on the list. Use every letter in the puzzle.

H	H	H	H
H	C	H	C
H	H	■	H
C	H	H	C
H	C	H	H

Hydrocarbon	Formula
methane	CH_4
ethane	C_2H_6
butane	C_4H_{10}
pentane	C_5H_{12}
hexane	C_6H_{14}

Now answer these questions:

a. If the dark square was an H, how would it change the answer?

_____

b. If the dark square was a C, how would it change the answer?

_____

2. *Hydrocarbon Models*: Draw circles (for Carbon or Hydrogen) to complete each of the following hydrocarbon molecular models. Place a *C* for *Carbon* and *H* for *Hydrogen* in the appropriate circle. How do you know where each label goes? CLUE:

Carbon (C) appears in the middle with pride,
while Hydrogen (H) "rests" to the far outside.
(See above model of methane gas.)

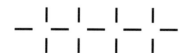

C_4H_{10} butane (gas)

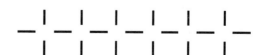

C_6H_{14} hexane (liquid)

PS–26
Metal Matter

Elements known as metals share several characteristics. Here are four common traits of a typical metal: (1) hard and shiny (solid and reflects light); (2) conducts heat and electricity; (3) malleable (can be hammered flat without breaking); and (4) ductile (can be drawn into a wire).

1. *Mental Metal:* How much do you know about metals? Try your luck with the following items. Circle the correct answer.

   a. Metals are usually found combined with other: (1) metals (2) ores (3) elements (4) corrosives.

   b. Metals are usually found in the form of compounds called: (1) elements (2) radicals (3) electrodes (4) ores.

   c. Metals have a silvery-gray color. These two do not: (1) tin, lead (2) gold, copper (3) aluminum, bronze (4) brass, iron.

   d. Some metals go through a chemical change known as: (1) reduction (2) replacement (3) inertia (4) corrosion.

   e. This metal is liquid at room temperature: (1) sodium (2) mercury (3) lead (4) zinc.

   f. Zinc is used to make brass. It comes from the mineral: (1) halite (2) bauxite (3) galena (4) sphalerite.

   g. Iron used by early humans came from: (1) steel (2) caves (3) meteorites (4) humus.

   h. Which is NOT TRUE for aluminum? (1) comes from bauxite (2) malleable (3) rare metal (4) chemical symbol: AL

   i. Which is NOT an example of a metal? (1) silicon (2) gold (3) sodium (4) copper

   j. Which is NOT an active metal? (1) sodium (2) magnesium (3) aluminum (4) tin

   k. The chemical symbol for copper is: (1) Co (2) Cu (3) Cp (4) Cr.

   l. This is an example of a light, tough silvery metal with a density of 1.7g/cm^3: (1) silver (2) platinum (3) magnesium (4) mercury.

   m. An excellent conductor of heat and electricity is: (1) copper (2) gypsum (3) sulfur (4) hydrogen.

   n. Hematite and magnetite are used in making: (1) brass (2) steel (3) copper (4) tin.

   o. Galena is used in making: (1) car batteries (2) bowls (3) cans (4) jewelry.

2. *More Ore Less:* An ore is a mineral or rock containing a valuable metal or nonmetal. Mineral example: iron ore; Nonmetallic example: sulfur ore.

   Brain Teaser: Metals must be removed from their ores before they can be used. How can zinc be removed from its carbonate ore ($ZnCO_3$) in 5 seconds or less?

PS–27
Alkali Metals

The alkali metals are located in the far left-hand column of the periodic table. These elements have a silver luster and serve as good conductors of heat and electricity. Each one is ductile and malleable.

Word Puzzle: Circle the word in the puzzle that completes each sentence below. Then write the word in the blanks. Answers may be up, down, forward, backward, or diagonal.

```
p  n  t  a  n  o  r  t  c  e  l  e
o  e  k  e  r  o  s  e  n  e  d  k
t  g  m  l  v  o  m  g  f  v  i  o
a  y  s  a  l  t  h  s  r  a  c  e
s  x  g  i  l  a  k  l  a  p  a  k
s  o  d  i  u  m  o  k  n  o  w  n
i  e  c  e  s  i  u  m  c  r  v  j
u  r  a  k  m  u  i  d  i  b  u  r
m  u  i  h  t  i  l  f  u  a  i  u
v  t  g  n  i  t  l  e  m  s  e  s
o  a  r  e  a  c  t  i  v  e  m  t
k  n  i  f  e  v  a  l  e  n  c  e
```

1. Each atom of an alkali metal has one _ _e_ _ r _ _ in its outermost shell.

2. K is the chemical symbol for _ _ _a_ _ _u_.

3. The alkali metal, _ _ _i_ _, is found in baking soda.

4. Alkali metals are _ _l_ _ at room temperature.

5. An a_ _ _ _ _ is a strong basic substance.

6. _r_ _ _i_ _ has 87 electrons.

7. _ _t_ _ _ _ has three protons and three electrons.

8. In their element form, the alkali metals are kept under k_ _ _s_ _ _. This keeps them from reacting with _x_ _____ or water v_ _ _ _ _ in the air.

9. Francium is the least k_ _ _ _ element of the alkali family.

10. Alkali metals have a low _e_ _ _n_ point.

11. Alkali metals are highly r_ _c_ _ _ _ _. Each atom of the alkali metals has only one v_ _ _n_ _ electron.

12. The soft alkali metals can be cut with a _ _i_ _.

13. Alkali metals are not found free in _a_ _ _ _ _.

14. _e_ _ _ _ _ is used in photoelectric cells.

PS–28
Metalloids

A. A metalloid is neither a metal nor a nonmetal. It's an element that has some of, but not all, the properties of metals. The following descriptions will help you identify six metalloids. The last letter for the name of each metalloid is given below. Use the letters in the box to spell the name of each element. Cross out a letter as you use it. Six letters will remain.

1. Chemical symbol between 1 and 15;   _ _ _ _ n
   used as plant food and weed killer.

2. Chemical symbol between 7 and 20;   _ _ _ _ _ _n
   pure element used in micro-electronic device.

3. Chemical symbol between 42 and 60;   _ _ _ _ _ _ _ _y
   mixed with lead in batteries.

4. Chemical symbol between 26 and 40;   _ _ _ _ _ _ _ _ _ m
   used in transistors.

5. Chemical symbol between 30 and 45;   _ _ _ _ _ _ _ c
   poisonous; some compounds used to
   make medicines; "Old Lace."

6. Chemical symbol between 48 and 59;   _ _ _ _ _ _ _ _ _ m
   used as a glass tint; alloying material.

e	b	r	i	e	u	l	t	z	o	g	u	i	l	m	i	o	n	i	s	a	c	t
a	n	r	u	a	o	s	a	n	g	e	n	z	i	r	i	g	l	o	m	r	i	

B. *Metalloid Puzzler:* Unscramble the six leftover letters in the box for the answer to this question: How would you describe the line separating the metals from the nonmetals in the Periodic Table of the Elements? HINT: Rhymes with "wig rag."

   Answer: _ _ _ _ _ _ line

C. *Another Metalloid Puzzler:* How does the following diagram describe a metalloid?

```
  metals
properties
 nonmetals
```

PS-29
Halogens

Halogens are a family of five nonmetallic chemical elements: Fluorine (F), Chlorine (Cl), Bromine (Br), Iodine (I), and Astatine (At). They have seven electrons in their outer shells. They are highly reactive with metals and form compounds called salts.

A. The right column lists features of elements in the halogen family. Match the features to the appropriate element in the left column. Place the feature's letter on the line inside the box. Write the letters in alphabetical order. Letters may apply to more than one element.

Features

1. Fluorine (F)

   _____

2. Chlorine (Cl)

   _____

3. Bromine (Br)

   _____

4. Iodine (I)

   _____

5. Astatine (At)

   _____

a. Forms ionic salts with metals
b. A solid
c. Has 53 electrons
d. A gas
e. Bleaching agent
f. Used in photographic film
g. Become ions
h. Radioactive; formed from bismuth
i. Has 35 protons and electrons
j. Can be obtained from seawater
k. Has 17 protons
l. Most highly reactive element
m. Forms greenish-yellow gas
n. Poisonous
o. Used to test for starch
p. Liquid (at room temperature)
q. Never found free in nature
r. Helps prevent tooth decay
s. Makes up part of table salt
t. Has 9 protons
u. Forms steel-gray crystals
v. Sublimates

B. *Halogen Family Riddle:* Mr. Bromine married Ms. Astatine. The had an "it." What kind of offspring did "it" turn out to be?

   Answer: "It" turned out to be a _____.

PS–30
Noble or Inert Gases

The elements located on the far right-side column of the periodic table form few compounds. These noble gases, as the name applies, remain chemically inactive. Why are these elements loners? Mostly because their electron shells are full, thus making them not too anxious to "bond with their neighbors."

1. *Solemn Column*: The six noble gases appear in a vertical column VIII (18) and have similar chemical properties. Use the clues to identify each gas and place it in its proper order in the column. NOTE: Do not refer to the periodic table. The elements appear with others in the box below.

   a. Do you want the one that fits in three?
      Then rearrange Miss "Nora G."

   b. "None" means nothing, but you can rearrange none into something. Where will it fit? One plus one's a hit!

   c. Five letters from "not oxygen" keep things alive. The proper letters give you number five.

   d. 2000 pounds with mixed r, K, y, and p put this between numbers five and three.

   e. The letters in "lie" and "hum" create the element for number one.

   f. Take a look, just for kicks; n + R make number six.

Xenon	Hydrogen
Oxygen	Helium
Radon	Argon
Thallium	Krypton
Neon	Nitrogen
Cobalt	Silicon

18
VIIIA

1

2

3

4

5

6

2. *Inert Puzzler:* Some noble gases have formed covalent compounds. Create a way to convert INERT into a compound. HINT: It has to do with potassium nitrate and sodium nitrate.

PS–31
Chemistry Term Puzzle

Find and circle the 18 terms needed to fill in the blanks. Terms may be up, down, forward, backward, or diagonal.

Terms	Clues
1. _ _ t _ _ _ s _	speeds up or slows down reaction
2. _ o _ _ _ u _ _	substance, two or more elements, chemically combined
3. _ _ l _ d _ _	simple salts, halogens
4. _ y _ _ _ l _ s _ _	chemical, water, both decompose
5. _ _ e _ _ _ o _	atom, negative unit
6. _ _ _ p _ _ _ t _ _ _	liquid ⟶ vapor
7. m _ _ _ b _ _ _ _ _	food ⟶ energy
8. _ _ l _	molecular weight, grams
9. _ n _ _ _	chemically inactive
10. _ s _ _ _ p _	same element, same atomic
11. s _ _ _ _ _ i _ _	number, different atomic weight
12. _ a _ _	mixture of solute and solvent
	crystals, NaCL
13. _ _ _ p _ _ _ _ t _ _ e	heat, measurement
14. _ i _ _ _ _ _ u _	22, element
15. r _ _ g _ _ _	chemical substance, produces chemical reaction
16. _ e _ _ d _ _ _	leftover, filtered solution
17. _ t _ _ _ u m	element, 39
18. _ _ a _ _	fermented sugars form alcohol and carbon dioxide

```
s  i  s  o  l  o  r  d  y  h  e  f  o  k  t
m  o  b  i  j  g  y  e  a  s  t  n  p  r  e
s  a  l  t  m  t  l  h  a  l  i  d  e  s  m
i  c  s  u  r  e  a  g  e  n  t  n  e  b  p
l  h  d  e  t  x  r  h  e  c  a  u  p  i  e
o  t  n  u  q  i  w  l  k  y  n  o  o  m  r
b  i  h  e  a  t  o  f  d  v  i  p  t  u  a
a  v  z  d  e  m  e  n  l  a  u  m  o  i  t
t  s  y  l  a  t  a  c  o  p  m  o  s  r  u
e  l  e  c  t  r  o  n  c  o  l  c  i  t  r
m  a  t  e  u  d  i  s  e  r  a  e  a  t  e
e  v  a  p  o  r  a  t  i  o  n  c  o  y  a
```

PS–32
Energy

A. Here are 20 terms related to energy, the ability to do work. Unfortunately, the vowels—a, e, i, o, u— are missing. Fill in the blanks with the missing vowels.

1. r _ _ c t _ _ _ n
2. p h _ t _ v _ l t _ _ _ c
3. c h _ m _ c _ l
4. t _ m p _ r _ t _ r _
5. _ l _ c t r _ c _ t y
6. s _ l _ r
7. p _ t _ n t _ _ _ l
8. k _ n _ t _ c
9. c _ t _ l y s t
10. _ n d _ t h _ r m _ c

11. _ n g _ n _
12. t _ r b _ n _
13. g _ s _ l _ n _
14. b _ n d _ n g
15. c _ m b _ s t _ _ n
16. n _ c l _ _ r
17. w _ t _ r
18. m _ c h _ n _ c _ l
19. _ l _ c t r _ m _ g n _ t _ c
20. g _ _ t h _ r m _ l

B. Match the numbers of eight terms from Part A with the following one-word clues. Place the number in the space to the right of the term.

steam   _____

earth   _____

sun   _____

atomic   _____

degrees   _____

liquid   _____

burning   _____

motion   _____

NOTE: If you total the numbers for the eight one-word examples, you should get (circle one)   94   95   96   97   98.

C. *Energy Puzzlers*:

1. Use the letters in ELECTROMAGNETIC to spell the names of two parts of an internal combustion engine. HINT 1: They help start the engine. HINT 2: One word rhymes with tuition; the other word rhymes with yellow. You may use a letter more than once.

2. Use the letters in ENERGETIC to spell the names of two different organisms. HINT: One hangs out in the jungle; the other is known as a "louse." You may use a letter more than once.

PS–33
Nuclear Energy

Nuclear energy is the energy released from an atom in nuclear reactions. This may occur in nuclear fission or nuclear fusion. Nuclear energy has been the source of much debate over the years. Safety is the key issue. This description only touches the surface of a powerful energy source. To learn a little bit more, you'll need to unscramble the statements below. The first one is done for you.

1. place the Nuclear sun reactions take in.
   Nuclear reactions take place in the sun.

2. two nuclei when fission into a breaks Nuclear more occurs or nucleus.

3. collide release and fusion, nuclei During energy two enormous.

4. reactions occur series of rapidly reaction is A very that chain a repeated.

5. neutron when atom A chain uranium of a begins is nucleus reaction bombarded the a with.

6. huge energy nuclei uranium split, As released are of neighboring quantities.

7. produce to energy electricity Nuclear used be can.

8. nuclear produced Electricity in from reactors nuclear energy is.

9. turns and steam The electricity turbines in generates nuclear reactors.

PS–34
Geothermal Energy

Geothermal energy comes from the heat within the Earth's interior. Find and circle 14 terms that relate in some way to geothermal energy. Use the clues listed below the puzzle. Write the puzzle terms in the blanks. Terms may be up, down, backward, forward, or diagonal.

```
C  E  N  T  I  G  R  A  D  E  R
R  X  D  N  A  L  E  C  I  E  F
U  P  S  C  O  O  K  R  N  V  Z
S  J  X  T  F  H  J  E  Y  I  P
T  F  H  J  E  Z  W  S  A  T  H
P  I  Q  A  F  A  Q  Y  C  C  T
N  Z  T  J  B  X  M  E  E  A  R
J  W  E  L  L  S  Q  G  D  F  A
T  N  E  M  N  O  R  I  V  N  E
```

Clues

1. _ _ _ _ _ are drilled deep to pump out hot water.

2. Power plants in _ _ _ _ _ _ _ _ (country) use geothermal energy.

3. Geothermal energy is used to _ _ _ _ buildings.

4. Geothermal energy is used to _ _ _ _ food.

5. A _ _ _ _ _ _ _ is a hot spring of boiling water.

6. The prefix "geo" refers to _ _ _ _ _ (rhymes with worth).

7. Hot gases and molten lava may come from _ _ _ _ _ _ _ volcanoes (opposite of sluggish).

8. Hot water and steam may reach a temperature of 350 degrees
   _ _ _ _ _ _ _ _ _ _ _.

9. Geothermal energy is a _ _e_ _ _w_ _ _ _e energy source.

10. Geothermal energy doesn't harm the _ _ _i_ _n_ _ _t.

11. Geothermal energy is used to generate electricity by _ _ _ _ _ _ (rhymes with dream) turbine-powered generators.

12. Geothermal heat may develop from certain movements of the Earth's _ _ _ _ _ _.

13. Some scientists believe natural nuclear _ _ _ _ _ _ (rhymes with delay) in the Earth's interior produces large amounts of heat.

14. Geothermal energy is generally tapped in areas where the Earth's crust is _ _ _ _ (rhymes with grin).

Name _____   Date _____

PS–35
Physical Change

Some substances continually undergo change. For example, if you smash a rock with a hammer, rock fragments fly everywhere. You've changed the size and shape of the rock. Even though the hammer altered the general appearance of the rock, the materials that formed it stayed the same. This is known as a physical change. Mixing, shrinking, and boiling are examples of physical change.

1. Ten more examples of a physical change are hidden in the puzzle. Circle the letters that spell the name of each physical change. Answers may be up, down, forward, backward, or diagonal.

```
a  f  m  e  g  n  i  z  e  e  r  f
g  b  a  t  n  n  j  h  i  s  b  g
n  g  n  w  o  c  i  n  g  t  r  n
i  n  g  i  r  e  g  t  e  g  n  i
v  i  l  s  t  f  c  a  l  x  h  h
l  l  i  t  u  o  r  g  k  e  i  c
o  p  n  i  e  i  u  n  r  n  m  t
s  m  g  n  n  e  s  i  g  s  p  e
s  u  a  g  g  b  h  y  m  f  z  r
i  r  c  n  y  t  i  v  a  r  g  t
d  c  i  h  p  v  n  s  w  c  e  s
b  e  n  d  i  n  g  e  d  o  n  a
```

Place the answers in alphabetical order.

_____

_____

_____

2. *Brain Twister:* This action can create a physical change:

   To break or release suddenly

   Use FOUR of the six underlined letters in PHYSICAL CHANGE to spell the term that matches the description above.

   — — — —

PS–36
Chemical Change

A chemical change occurs when one substance changes into another. The new substance appears different. For example, when bread pops out of a toaster, the dark crunchy bread has lost its original white color and soft texture. Bread turns into toast. A chemical change has taken place.

1. Each of the following items undergoes a chemical change. In the column labeled CHEMICAL CHANGE, give an example of a change that takes place. The first one is done for you.

Item	Chemical Change . . .
a. firecracker (solid) . . .	explodes (gases)
b. burned sugar changes into . . .	
c. sweet milk changes into . . .	
d. decaying plants turn into . . .	
e. old iron nail forms . . .	
f. 3-month-old egg turns . . .	
g. burnt hot dog turns into . . .	
h. burned paper produces . . .	
i. gastric digestion of food becomes . . .	

2. Circle the letters in the box that spell the capitalized words in each statement below. Use the remaining letters to fill in the blanks in the statement under the box.

   • Vinegar mixed with baking soda produce CARBON DIOXIDE.

   • Rusting iron produces IRON OXIDE.

D	C	I	P	O	T	N	S	R	O	S	D
O	E	R	H	B	D	H	X	T	I	S	I
I	N	E	O	I	X	A	N	O	E	Y	O

   The food-making, chemical change process in plants
   is known as _ _ _ _ _ _ _ _ _ _ _ _ _ _.

3. Chemical changes are associated with (a) _ _ _ _ _ _ _ changes. These may occur in the form of (b) _ _ _ _, (c) _ _ _ _ _ _, (d) _ _ _ _ _, or electrical energy.

   Use the following hints to help you fill in the blanks with the appropriate terms: (a) the ability to do work; produces change in matter. (b) moving molecules produce this; a type of energy. (c) a form of energy; travels 186,000 miles per second. (d) auditory sensation; a form of energy.

Name _____   Date _____

PS–37
Compound Water

A. The compound water is composed of hydrogen and oxygen. The following facts concerning water are incomplete. Some letters are missing from each statement. Supply the missing letters, locate the word in the puzzle, and draw a circle around it. The words in the puzzle may be up, down, backward, forward, or diagonal.

1. Water exists as a __o__i__, __i__ui__, and __a__.

2. Water e__ __and__ as it freezes.

3. Water makes an excellent so__ __en__ because it does not break up or de__ __mp__se easily.

4. Water fit to drink is known as p__ __ab__e water.

5. __ol__ __ted water is unfit for living organisms and harms the environment.

6. The d__ __til__ati__ __ process purifies water.

7. Water pressure increases with __ep__h.

8. There is twice as much __ __d__o__en in water as __ __y__en.

9. Distilled water is a poor c o__ __uc__or of electricity.

10. Covalent bonding occurs when two atoms share electrons. Water, a covalent __o__po__n__, shares electrons.

11. Water has a sp__ __if__c __ra__ __ty (2 words) of one.

12. Below zero degrees __en__ig__a__e water is either ice or snow.

13. Water becomes __ __ea__ when the temperature climbs above one hundred degrees centigrade.

```
s p e c i f i c u o x g c t
h e d a r g i t n e c r o l
y d e c o m p o s e k a m s
d p o t a b l e i a y v p a
r j s w e q d e p t h i o m
o a x s a i d i c a s t u a
g o a y u t p y e o x y n e
e b w q t n e v l o s g d t
n o i t a l l i t s i d c s
r l j z q s d n a p x e v s
p o l l u t e d m e t a l o
e t e r o t c u d n o c i x
f a h n e g y x o w a r r e
```

B. *Water Puzzler*: Create two different water conditions from these 14 letters:

   t   r   H   H   H   H   O   o   O   d   s   h   a   f

PS–38
Compound Maze

A. A compound is a substance composed of two or more different elements that are chemically combined. Ten examples of compounds are hidden in the maze below. Circle each example and write it on the space under the puzzle. Then draw a line through the Compound Maze. Start your search at the maze entrance. Your line should extend from the entrance to the exit and run through the circled words. In some words, the line will pass through only parts of a word. The answers appear horizontally, vertically, or diagonally, and either backwards or forwards. Use the chemical formulas in parentheses to help you find the answers.

```
ENTRANCE ──▶ w a t e r t n i c k e l a i
             u e s b g a m u n i t a l p
             t k u o f i s a r k v q h c
             c a r b o n d i o x i d e o
             n e d z n o t p y r k a z b
             o n l a i m e t h a n e p a
             n i o e p m j d k y c l o l
             e d g i b a k i n g s o d a
             x o l e u r m u i d a r n r
             n i k e t p c x z w l i a e
             e s u g a r a d o n t s m v
             s a m a n g a n e s e u w l
             u n j h e v e n i m o r b i
             l d x b i n e t s g n u t s
                 ▲
                  \  EXIT
```

1. _____ (C + O + O)   6. _____ (SiO$_2$)

2. _____ (C$_{12}$H$_{22}$O$_{11)}$)   7. _____ (NaCL)

3. _____ (H + H + O)   8. _____ (NH$_3$)

4. _____ (NaHCO$_3$)   9. _____ (C$_4$H$_{10}$)

5. _____ (CH$_4$)   10. _____ (Fe$_2$O$_3$)

B. *Compound Puzzler*: Unscramble the following letters and number to create a compound:

$$m \ + \ 16\,oz \ + \ c \ + \ o$$

PS–39
Solutions

Solutions are mixtures of two or more substances that mix evenly with each other.

1. *Liquid Solutions*: A solid may dissolve in a liquid to form a liquid solution. Shade in the letters that spell the names of four mystery solids capable of forming liquid solutions. The letters appear in order.

a. water + | g | s | e | a | w | r | l | o | t | c | b | i |

b. water + | e | c | s | k | u | o | g | d | a | i | f | r |

c. water + | g | c | h | u | l | v | o | r | i | y | n | f | e | k | t | a | j | b | l | m | e | t | s |

   Hint: water purification

d. water + | i | A | h | k | n | a | B | S | o | e | l | F | t | z | C | e | m | p | r | O | v | i |

   Hint: medicine

2. *The S Word Puzzle*: All of the terms in the puzzle begin with the letter s. Use the clues to guide you in completing the puzzle.

ACROSS:

3. a mixture that settles on standing
4. a solution holding maximum solute
6. essential part of solution
7. sweet substance
8. able to dissolve
10. the substance in which a solute dissolves

DOWN:

1. a substance that dissolves in a solution
2. to take away from a mixture
5. up, down, back, forth, and so on
6. results of dissolving a solute in a solvent
8. sodium chloride
9. particles coming to rest

PS–40
Acids and Bases

1. An acid is a substance in solution that yields hydrogen ions. Examples of acids: acetic, citric, hydrochloric, and sulfuric. A base is a substance that yields hydroxide ions in solution. Examples of bases: ammonia water, lye, and calcium hydroxide.

   Mr. Ion, science teacher, asked Tony to taste two WEAK acid and base solutions. He then had Tony perform a litmus paper test on each solution.

   DRAW Tony's facial expressions after testing the acid and base solutions. Also indicate the color change on the litmus paper. Use DOTS for RED and X's for BLUE.

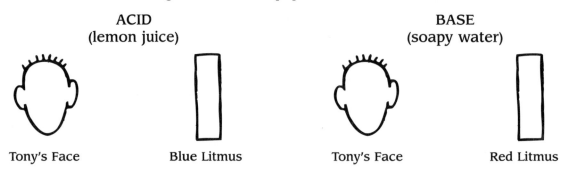

ACID (lemon juice)		BASE (soapy water)	
Tony's Face	Blue Litmus	Tony's Face	Red Litmus

2. Circle the four true statements.
   a. All acid compounds contain hydrogen.
   b. Acids taste salty, feel sticky.
   c. A pH reading of 3.0 indicates acid.
   d. Acids have little commercial use.
   e. A pH of 7 indicates a strong base solution.
   f. An acid can react with a base to form a salt.
   g. The term alkali refers to strong bases.
   h. All substances that contain hydrogen are acids.

3. Place an A for ACID or B for BASE on the line before each statement.
   ____ conducts electricity
   ____ solution containing H+ ions
   ____ pH greater than 7
   ____ sour taste
   ____ a pH of 3.5
   ____ corrosive; "eats away" metals
   ____ produces hydroxide ions in solution
   ____ bitter taste

4. *Brain Blaster:* What is a chemist's favorite outdoor sport?

PS-41
Scrambled Facts About Forces

A. These 10 jumbled statements regarding forces need to be unscrambled. Write the unscrambled statements on the lines.

1. force Work distance equals times.

   _____

2. objects slows moving Frictional down force.

   _____

3. size are direction in forces opposite Balanced equal and in.

   _____

   _____

4. object changes on force the net velocity object A always an the of.

   _____

   _____

5. motion Newton's forces describe laws the three of effect of.

   _____

   _____

6. measure gravity of weight of force The object the of an the is.

   _____

   _____

7. pushes forces All or pulls are.

   _____

8. Electromagnetic atoms together molecules forces hold and.

   _____

   _____

9. when objects pushes force Buoyancy that they fluid a is on a placed up are in.

   _____

   _____

10. called surface upon Force is acting area pressure a of unit.

    _____

    _____

B. *Force Puzzler*: Momentum is the product of velocity and mass; the driving force behind a moving object. In an active family, what member represents nearly 38 percent of the momentum?

PS–42
Four-Letter Forces Puzzle

A. A force may be described as a push or pull that is exerted on matter. For example, a wind force of 60-plus knots can uproot trees. Use the clues below to help you fill in the spaces with force or force-related terms.

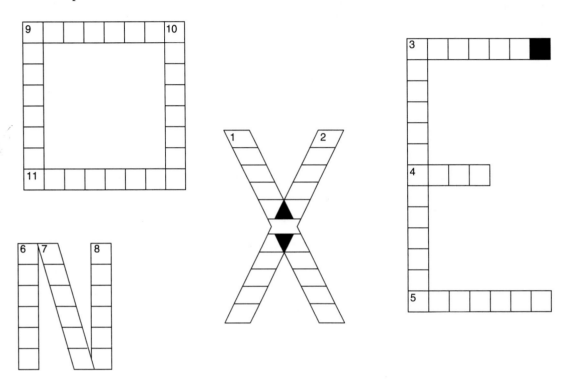

Clues: 1. Inward force, pulls body out of a straight-line path; 2. Outward force, pulls body away from the center of revolution; 3. (*across*) The amount of force expressed in terms of 32 feet/second per second; 3. (*down*) The force behind the attraction between the Earth and all objects on it; 4. An abbreviation for the strength of an electric current; 5. A force responsible for bringing something up to a higher position; 6. Forward force of a propeller, for example; 7. Product of force and the perpendicular distance for a fulcrum; 8. Any quantity (force) that has magnitude (amount) and direction; 9. (*across, backwards*) A force possessing electrons and protons; 9. (*down, backwards*) A repelling or attracting force; 10. To apply a source of electromotive force; 11. To equip with a motor

B. *Force Puzzler:* Rearrange the four letters in the puzzle to produce a "bovid ruminant draft mammal." __ __ __ __

PS–43
Time for Work

A. Find and shade in the 10 terms related to work. Place each darkened term in the space next to its hint in parentheses. The words can be found up, down, forward, or backward.

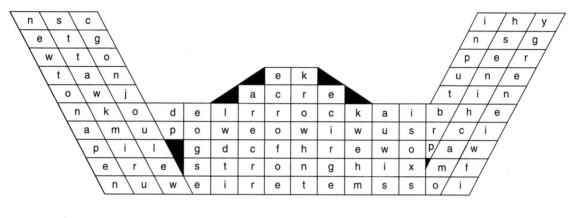

_____	(push or pull)
_____	(work requires this)
_____	(lifting weights, for example)
_____	(force measurement)
_____	(distance measurement)
_____	(speed up work)
_____	(amount of effort)
_____	(rate of work)
_____	(one newton-meter)
_____	(measurement of power)

B. *Work Puzzlers*:

1. Mary and Joy went to the gym for a morning workout. Mary lifted 10-pound weights with both hands for 15 minutes. Joy held a 50-pound weight over her head for two minutes. Which girl, Mary or Joy, did more work? Explain your answer.

   _____

   _____

2. If you blow a feather two feet up in the air, are you doing any work? Explain your answer.

   _____

   _____

3. How does the nonsensical word "diosbtjaenccte" describe work? Be careful!

   _____

   _____

169

Name _____   Date _____

PS–44
Machines, Part 1

A machine is a device that changes the amount, speed, or direction of a force.

Four-Sided Puzzles: Complete the four sides of each figure with a word related in some way to machines. The answers may appear forward, backward, horizontally, or vertically. Use the clues to help you complete each puzzle.

Puzzle One

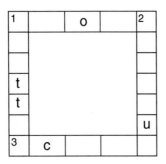

ACROSS
1. Example of third-class level
3. Exerting a push or pull

DOWN
1. Hard, inflexible machine
2. A lever pivots on this

Puzzle Two

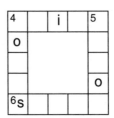

ACROSS
4. Class of a lever
6. A simple machine

DOWN
4. Example of third-class lever
5. Machines are found all around the _____

Puzzle Three

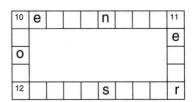

ACROSS
7. Made up of two or more simple machines (2 words)
9. Fulcrum between effort and resistance (3 words)

DOWN
7. Example of a first-class lever
8. Short tube for tightening a joint

Puzzle Four

ACROSS
10. Skill in using machines
12. Opposition to force

DOWN
10. Antlered mammal machine
11. Pry bar machine

© 2001 by The Center for Applied Research in Education

170

PS–45
Machines, Part 2

A. There are 20 terms related to machines that are missing three or more letters. The missing parts of the terms are hidden in the puzzle. Find and circle the missing letters. Then place them in the blanks next to the partial terms.

p	o	u	n	d	z	b	s	v	e
t	i	o	n	e	e	d	i	e	c
p	e	c	r	u	m	f	s	r	t
u	a	h	d	i	r	d	t	i	i
t	l	j	g	r	c	e	a	e	o
o	k	m	e	r	q	z	n	n	n
r	o	n	d	p	u	t	c	c	f
t	r	s	t	k	l	l	e	y	s
b	f	h	j	w	e	r	q	x	b

1. i n _ _ _
2. e f f _ _ _
3. f i _ _ _
4. w e _ _ _
5. f u l _ _ _ _
6. c o m _ _ _ _ _
7. f r i c _ _ _ _
8. r e _ _ _ _ _ _ _ _
9. e f f i c _ _ _ _ _
10. t h _ _ _

11. i d _ _ _
12. s p _ _ _ _
13. l e _ _ _ _
14. d i r _ _ _ _ _ _ _
15. p u _ _ _ _ _
16. h a m _ _ _ _
17. s e c _ _ _ _
18. f o _ _ _
19. o u t _ _ _
20. p o _ _ _

B. Match eight answers from Part A with their descriptions given below. Place the letter of the description on the line.

Items from Part A

___ 16
___ 15
___ 4
___ 18
___ 8
___ 1
___ 20
___ 13

Descriptions

a. a push or pull
b. force against motion
c. bar; machine
d. strength of force
e. first-class lever
f. amount of effort
g. fixed or movable
h. inclined plane

Name _____ Date _____

PS–46
Newton's First Law of Motion

Sir Isaac Newton, English scientist, described the laws of gravity and motion. His first law of motion states that an object at rest tends to remain at rest; a moving object keeps moving at the same speed and in the same direction.

1. *Stubborn Object*: An object resists any change in motion. If motionless, it remains still; if moving, it continues to move. Newton had a name for this mulelike resistance. To discover the name, decode and unscramble the symbols, letters, and sketches.

 + n + 1st letter in English alphabet + e +

 "fore" + i + 18th letter in English alphabet

   Answer: __ __ __ __ __ __ __

2. *On the Move*: A fast-moving car tends to keep going straight as it rounds a curve. Sketch what this looks like in the box. Briefly explain why this is an example of Newton's first law.

   [box]

   This is an example of Newton's first law because _____

   _____

   _____

3. *Sudden Change*: A moving body tends to go in a straight line. Find and circle the items in the puzzle that change the direction of these moving objects: a. pitched baseball (2 words), b. tennis ball, c. running back (football), d. dart (2 words), e. ping-pong ball. Answers may be up, down, forward, backward, or diagonal.

```
r  e  k  c  a  b  e  n  i  l
d  a  r  t  b  o  a  r  d  s
w  v  c  l  p  q  n  u  k  z
i  y  j  k  i  c  b  t  w  m
a  i  t  g  e  l  d  d  a  p
t  a  b  l  a  t  e  m  x  o
```

4. *"Kookie" Riddle:* What is a "pear-shaped container of seedlike fruits de Isaac"?

Name _____   Date _____

PS–47
Newton's Second Law of Motion

Newton's second law of motion states that for a given mass, the greater the force, the greater the acceleration. The object (mass) accelerates in the direction of the applied force.

1. *Come to Terms*

    a. FORCE—a push or pull on an object. Circle the items that can create movement.

    hands   rocks   wind   feet   rope   insects

    b. MASS—the amount of matter in an object. Circle the items that have mass.

    books   volleyball   rat   wire   leg   vacuum

    c. ACCELERATION—how fast an object changes its velocity (speed and direction of travel). Circle the items that show acceleration.

    rocket   hockey player   molecules at -273° C   rain

2. *Newton, Anyone?*: A newton (N) is a unit of force or weight. A newton is the force needed to give a one-kilogram (kg) mass an acceleration of one meter per second per second (1m/s/s). Newton's second law of motion may be expressed as follows:

    Force = mass × acceleration

    A baseball has a mass of 0.75 kg. It travels 85 meters. How much force was needed? _____N

3. *Force Yourself*: Use the letters below to answer this question: What is the FORCE behind Newton's laws?

    p   s   l   o   p   r   u   u   l   h

    The force is a _____.

4. *Riddle Rap:* What state in the U.S. ALWAYS features part of Newton's second law of motion?

© 2001 by The Center for Applied Research in Education

173

PS–48
Newton's Third Law of Motion

Newton's third law states that for every force, there is an equal and opposite force; for every action, there is an equal and opposite reaction. So with every force exerted, an equal force will be exerted in the opposite direction. *Example:* Two bumper cars hit head on. The impact causes both cars to bounce backward. This shows how forces act in pairs or how an action–reaction occurs. The two cars hit each other and are pushed away at the same time.

1. *Action–Reaction Satisfaction*: Identify the ACTION and REACTION for each situation. Write your answers on the lines.

   a. Walking on Cement

      ACTION: _____

      REACTION: _____

   b. Rowing a Boat

      ACTION: _____

      REACTION: _____

   c. A Rocket Blasting Off

      ACTION: _____

      REACTION: _____

2. *Find Five*: Locate and circle in the puzzle five objects that can be used to demonstrate Newton's third law. Answers may be up, down, forward, backward, or diagonal.

   ```
   s h c d e o b
   k i q m c a v
   a r i f l e m
   t g x l g y l
   e p o r t a l
   u o s u k v a
   n w c z d h b
   ```

3. *Too Many Forces*: You can create FORCES by writing the same letter four times. Try it. *Answer:* __ __ __ __ = FORCES.

4. *Rotund Riddle:* Where did gravity exert the most force on Newton? (*Hint:* The force of gravity acting on a body produces weight.)

Name _____   Date _____

PS–49
Heat

Heat is a form of energy. Heat energy keeps molecules in constant motion. The molecules move faster as heat energy increases.

Write the answers to the numbered clues in the space provided. These answers will give you the words to complete the crossword puzzle. The crossword contains letter clues to help you place the words.

1. Heat travels through _____ by conduction.
2. All forms of energy can be changed to heat _____.
3. In _____, heat energy transfers through empty space by waves.
4. The amount of heat needed to raise the temperature of one gram of water one Celsius degree is known as _____.
5. Molecules in motion have _____ energy.
6. _____ occurs when heat is transferred by the movement of flowing gases or liquids.
7. Heat passes very slowly through an _____.
8. A heat _____ is a machine that changes heat into mechanical energy.
9. A steam _____ is an example of number eight above.
10. A gram of pure solid substance needs a certain amount of heat to melt completely. This amount is known as heat of _____.
11. The measurement of how cold or hot an object is refers to _____.
12. The burning of coal is a chemical _____ that releases heat energy.
13. Heat causes substances to _____.

PS–50
Physical Science Puzzlers

Here are 10 puzzlers to sharpen your creative-thinking power.

1. Use the letters in "wreetch" to produce three different words. Make "heat" part of each word. RULE: You must use all seven letters in "wreetch."

        heat   heat   heat

2. Produce a common chemical compound from the word CRYSTAL. You don't need to use all seven letters.

3. Where would you find the MOST force in pressure?

4. Show how the "gravitational force that Earth exerts on an object" can be produced from the following:

        1 + 2 + 3 + 2 + 23rd letter in the English alphabet

5. Some elements should NEVER mix with living organisms. For example, what would happen if too much *As* got into *U*?

6. Create a simple way to convert a nonmetal into a metal.

7. Show a way to illustrate matter in space using only letters.

8. Show, using a diagram, how three different metals—IRON, NICKEL, and COBALT—are attracted to a magnet.

9. The deeper an object goes under water, the greater the water pressure. Show this principle with a diagram using the words WATER, LOW PRESSURE, and HIGH PRESSURE.

10. Show underwater sound using the word SOUND and six w's.

Name _____   Date _____

PS–51
Electricity

1. Match the term with the two-word description. Place the letter of the description on the appropriate line.

Term	Description
_____ current	a. friction, electrons
_____ series circuit	b. electron, proton
_____ ampere	c. electron flow
_____ lightning	d. separate branches
_____ ohms	e. atmospheric electricity
_____ parallel circuit	f. measures current
_____ static electricity	g. one path
_____ electrical field	h. electrical resistance

2. Look at Figure A and Figure B. The word "charges" in each figure represents electrical particles. Why do the particles in Figure B attract each other?

    charges + charges = repel   ChArGeS + cHaRgEs = attract
    Figure A   *Figure B*

3. When an object has neither a positive nor a negative electric charge, the object is neutral. Count the number of positive (+) and negative (–) charges in the object below. Is the object negatively charged, positively charged, or neutral? Explain your answer.

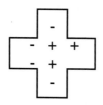

4. Electricity produced from a power source lit 15 street lamps for six months. One night ALL the lamps failed to light. What happened? The illustration offers a clue.

    power source   **electr . . . . .**   **15 street lamps**

5. *Brain Shocker:* What does (e) represent?

    (a)   c   i   r   c   u   i   t
    (b)   c   i   r   c   u   i   t
    (c)   c   i   r   c   u   i   t
    (d)   c   i   r   c   u   i   t
    (e)   circuit

PS–52
Magnetism

1. The letters that represent the chemical symbols of three metals attracted to a magnet appear below. They are mixed with the letters that spell magnet. Unscramble the letters and place them in the diagram.

g   N   o   n   C   i   F   a   m   e   t   e

symbols

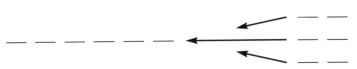

2. If you bring a powerful magnet near a small block of wood, the wood WILL NOT be attracted to the magnet. The magnet WILL NOT lift the wood. However, YOU CAN pick up the wood with two weak magnets. How can this be done?

3. Place a T for TRUE or F for FALSE in the space to the left of each statement.

    _____ a. Alnico is a natural substance attracted to magnets.

    _____ b. Lodestone, found in nature, is a natural magnet.

    _____ c. An artificial magnet has a north pole and a south pole.

    _____ d. The south pole of a magnet attracts the south pole of another magnet.

    _____ e. The behavior of magnetic poles is known as the Law of Polarity.

    _____ f. The visible lines in the magnetic field are called lines of force.

    _____ g. An electric current can produce a magnetic field around a wire.

    _____ h. A magnetic substance can be made into a magnet by stroking the substance with a magnet.

4. As Dan and Rosa walked by a jewelry store window, Dan stopped and pointed to an expensive bracelet. He asked Rosa, "What would you like for your birthday?" Rosa hesitated while gazing at the bracelet. A smile crossed her lips. Finally, she answered, "I'd like something made of metal, a little different, and, most of all, attractive." What do you think Dan gave Rosa?

5. *Brain Strainer:* Why did Leonard carry a horseshoe magnet in his pocket?

PS–53
Sound

1. Sound is a form of energy produced by vibrating matter. Sound waves travel through solid, liquid, or gas. Show, by connecting ends 1 and 2 with a line on the illustration below, how sound travels through matter.

```
           s    c    r    r    h
   (1)     h    l    u    a    y
           a    o    b    i    d
           l    u    b    n    r    (2)
           e    d    e         o
                s    r         g
                               e
                               n
```

matter

2. Vibrating matter stimulates the auditory nerves and allows us to hear sounds. The vibrations spread out in all directions and travel through space as sound waves. Unscramble the names of six 2-word LOUD NOISE PRODUCERS.

Scrambled Letters	Loud Noise Producers	
a. ewrop orewm	_____	_____
b. ocrk csmiu	_____	_____
c. nrugyh abby	_____	_____
d. etj ngeien	_____	_____
e. nahic wsa	_____	_____
f. ubneacmal srien	_____	_____

3. Sounds carry different pitches. You can identify different animals by the sounds they make. Circle the seven animal sounds in the group of letters. Go from left to right.

```
t r a b a a f l i m w h i n n y d o h i s s b k p u r r t
a m b e w o o f b e r s c a w t h e c h i r p o w h i t e
```

4. A ship may detect a submarine, the depth of the ocean, and the location of fish. Show, using the words and line below, how the ship is able to do this.

sound, water _____

5. Sound travels a mile (5,280 feet) in about 5 seconds. How long would it take sound to travel 3 miles across the surface of the moon?

PS-54
Light

Light is a form of energy. It acts upon the retina and optic fibers of the eye making sight possible. Therefore, thanks to light, we see many things.

1. Use the three clues to identify the "thing" associated with light. Write the answer in the spaces.

    a.   image, dark, silhouette   _ _ _ _ o _

    b.   sun, moon, earth   _ _ _ i _ _ _ _

    c.   smooth, image, silver   _ i _ _ _ _ _

    d.   image, lens, Ceres   _ _ _ e _ _ _ _ _ _

    e.   water, transparent, bend   _ _ _ r _ _ _ _ _ _ _

    f.   false, illusion, floating   _ _ _ a _ _ _

    g.   beam, glass, prism   _ _ _ c _ _ _ _ _

2. What is wrong with this picture?

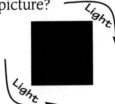

3. Light travels about 186,000 miles per second. The sun is 93 million miles from Earth. How many minutes does it take light to reach us from the sun?

4. If you hold up a book to a mirror, all the letters are backwards. Write the word OHIO on a piece of paper. Hold a mirror horizontal to the letters. How could you PROVE that the letters are backwards?

5. Materials that block all light are called opaque. Fill in the blanks with letters that spell the names of opaque objects commonly found in most banks.

    _ o _ n _

    p _ o _ l _

    _ a _ e _

    q _ _ r _ e _ _

    _ _ u l _ _ _

    _ e _ n _ e _

6. *Brain Squeezer:* How much does light weigh? Describe a way to weigh light.

PS–55

Light: Reflection, Part 1

Light may strike a smooth surface and bounce back. We refer to this as reflection. Let's take a closer look at this bending or throwing back of light.

A. *Good Reflection*: A smooth shiny surface, like a mirror, reflects most of the light in one direction. The reflected light goes to your eye. Reflected light follows the law of reflection which states that the angle of incidence (light striking an object) is equal to the angle of reflection (light bouncing away). Use a ruler, protractor, and pencil to draw the angle of reflection for each diagram below. The normal (perpendicular) line forms a 90-degree angle. This line will help you determine the angle of the reflected ray. Write the degrees for each angle of reflection under the diagrams.

1.

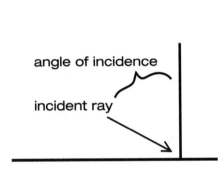

angle of reflection: _____ **degrees**

2.

angle of reflection: _____ **degrees**

3.

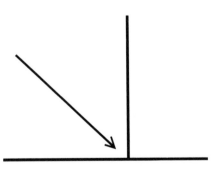

angle of reflection: _____ **degrees**

4.

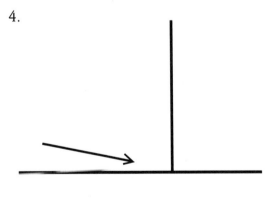

angle of reflection: _____ **degrees**

B. *Smooth Sailing*: The scrambled letters spell the names of two smooth surfaces known to reflect light. Identify them.

1. wdeax   gmy   orolf   _____

2. lmac   rcale   keal   _____

PS–56
Light: Reflection, Part 2

A. *Rough and Tumble*: How does light reflect from a bumpy or uneven surface? Regardless of the texture of the surface, light bounces away after it makes contact. The light follows the law of reflection (See Light: Reflection, Part 1). However, irregular reflection, or diffusion (scattering of light rays), occurs when light strikes a round surface. For example:

Use a ruler, protractor, and pencil to show how the light ray will be reflected by the following rough surface.

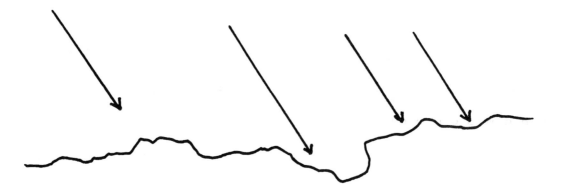

B. *Mirror Delight*: A light ray can be reflected several times from shiny smooth surfaces. Use a ruler, protractor, and pencil to show how the ray will be reflected by the three mirrors.

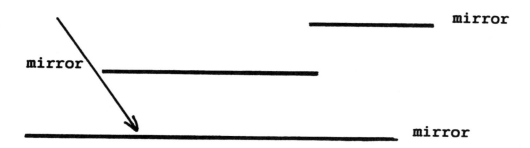

Name _____   Date _____

PS–57
Light: Refraction

Refraction is the bending of a beam of light as it moves from one medium to another. The diagram below gives an example of light being refracted as it travels through glass. Light bends because the glass medium acts as a cushion and slows it down.

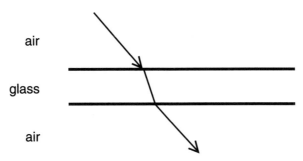

air

glass

air

Bend a Little: Circle EVERY OTHER LETTER in the series of letters below. Then unscramble the letters to form a word associated with refraction of light. Write the word on the line.

Scrambled Letters	Clues
1. n a t g w s i l e s p	dense medium
2. t r s a p i	thin medium
3. a e w s c n o l i s y e v	form images
4. d e g t j n q b w	light condition
5. i m w e p r c t m p s c k u d s	bent rays
6. w e f r h d g	least refracted
7. a s l r q i b p z m o	separates light
8. c t r o g e k i o l y v d	most refracted
9. i m n a q a s r t e a c g	refraction device
10. s d l x c e y n v i p	refracting ability
11. o u s u t a p m a v x c n	smallest index
12. g d e n y a w i b d s m l o r	large index

PS–58
Color

Color may be described as the property of light determined by its wavelength. An object's color depends on the color of light that it reflects. Conversely, a black object absorbs most of the light that shines on it.

1. *Where There's an E*: Use the three-word clues to help you identify the words related in some way to color. Each word has at least one e.

		Three-Word Clues
a.	_ e _ _ e _ _	bouncing back, light
b.	_ _ _ _ _ e _ e _ _ _ _ _	two colors, white
c.	_ _ _ e _	retina, color sensitive
d.	_ _ e _ _ _ _ _	light, seven colors
e.	_ _ _ _ e _ _	coloring matter, mixed
f.	_ _ _ _ e	prism, spectrum, light
g.	_ _ e	color name, distinct
h.	_ _ _ _ e	color, degree, darkness
i.	_ _ _ e	quality, tint, color
j.	_ _ _ _ _ _ e _	not reflected, black
k.	_ e _	light, least refracted
l.	_ _ _ _ e _	light, most refracted
m.	_ _ e _ _ e _ _ _	color, depends on

2. *Color Challenge*: Try to make a list of eight different colors from the letters in the box in five minutes or less. You may use a letter more than once.

r	a	b	k	u	l	c	e	v	n	o	g	p	i	t	d

_____   _____

_____   _____

_____   _____

_____   _____

Name _____   Date _____

PS–59
Physical Science Mini-Problems

1. It is extremely important to make careful measurements when handling chemicals in an experiment. Circle the letters in a term below that completes the following sentence:

    Accuracy counts because you want to be _____.

millimeter	metric	balance	alkaline
satellite	solvent	measure	alloy
experiment	evaporate	buoyant	metalloid

2. As you read the message, cross out the letters in CIRCUMFERENCE.

    "The third letters of the alphabet must go. Remove the e's, too! Bye, bye, to the i. Go ahead and cross out the r's. Last, eliminate the m."

    If everything went well, the remaining three letters (unscrambled) will spell out what this activity should have been.

    This activity should have been __ __ __.

3. See if you can complete the names of three different insects using the letters in CENTIGRAM. You may use a letter more than once.

    a. __ n __
    b. __ n __ __
    c. __ __ __ n __   fly

4. The box contains two-, three-, and four-letter combinations. Combine six of them to spell the names of THREE PHYSICAL PROPERTIES of matter.

hard	cal	sol	sity	ne	sub	ness
den	mag	ubi	col	sium	or	lity

    a. _____   b. _____   c. _____

5. List the names of 10 fruits using the letters in PERIODIC TABLE OF ELEMENTS to create the words. A letter may be used more than once.

6. Use your creative energy to unscramble the letters to produce an example of energy of motion.

two i's,	three e's,	two n's,	one k,	one t,	one c,
	one g,	one r,	one y		

    An example of energy of motion is _____.

PS-60
More Physical Science Mini-Problems

1. Mrs. Celsius, science teacher, enjoyed creating problems and riddles to spring on her classes. She told her students that temperature can be measured in centimeters. How do you think she could demonstrate this to her students?

   _____

   _____

2. Mrs. Celsius never stops! She said temperature can also be measured in yards. Create a way to do this.

   _____

   _____

3. Show how SIX elements properly arranged can produce friction.

   _____

   _____

4. You have three blocks. They are B R U .   Show, using an arrow, how you can arrange the blocks to produce friction. Also, briefly explain your strategy.

   _____

   _____

   _____

   _____

5. Use the letters in HEAT ENERGY to spell the names of three items:
   a. a drink _____
   b. a domestic animal _____
   c. a wild animal _____

6. List six terms related to force and motion that have a "ti" combination in their names.
   a. _____
   b. _____
   c. _____
   d. _____
   e. _____
   f. _____

Answer Key

Earth Science

ES–1. EARTH SCIENTISTS

1. earth, 2. earthquakes, 3. maps, 4. layers, 5. ponds, 6. universe, 7. crust, forces,
8. cities, artifacts, 9. rocks, 10. past life

Bonus Challenge Answer: A person who studies the waters of the earth is a hydrologist.

ES–2. HERE ON EARTH, PART 1

1. f, 2. d, 3. i, 4. g, 5. c, 6. b, 7. h, 8. e, 9. a, 10. j

ES–3. HERE ON EARTH, PART 2

1. g, 2. b, 3. c, 4. h, 5. j, 6. i, 7. f, 8. d, 9. e, 10. a

ES–4. EARTH HAPPENINGS

1. mudflow   2. erosion   3. earthquake   4. dormant volcano
5. moraine   6. fossil   7. stalactite   8. tsunami

ES–5. MAPPING

1. False items: b, d, f, g

2. a.   b.   c.   d.    e.

f.    g.

3.

ES-6. SPACE OBJECTS

1. frozen gases, dust (or rock), rock (or dust)
2. Comet X because Comet Y is too far from the Earth. It has a large elliptical orbit around the Sun.
3. a. meteoroid,   b. meteor,   c. meteorite
4. planoid, solar, planet, belt, orbits, rock, iron, diameter

ES-7. SUN TIME

1. never,   2. energy,   3. Mars,   4. star,   5. diameter,   6. hydrogen,   7. velocity,
8. humid,   9. solar,   10. (sun)spots,   11. rays

```
s t a r
o               h u m i d        v
l               y        i       e
a               d        a       l
r a y s         r        m       o
        p       o        e       c
        o       g        t       i
        t       e        e       t
M a r s         n e v e r        y g r e n e
```

Riddle: They are called a solar panel.

ES-8. MOON THINGS

ACROSS: 2. sunlight,   3. craters,   5. rills,   8. maria,   9. revolves,   11. Copernicus,
13. meteorites
DOWN: 1. albedo,   4. satellite,   6. eclipse,   7. perigee,   10. support,   12. sixth

ES-9. PLANET MERCURY

1. The X should be about 3.6 centimeters (nearly 1.5 inches) from the sun.
2. Answers will vary. Mercury orbits the sun in 88 days. Mercury, a messenger, represents speed or quickness.
3. moon or atmosphere
4. a. lead,   b. magnetic,   c. craters,   d. orbits,   e. terrestrial
5. Names will vary.
6. Because Mercury has always been close to the sun

ES-10. PLANET VENUS

1. The X should be about 6.7 centimeters (nearly 2.75 inches) from the sun.
2. a. phases,   b. greenhouse,   c. dioxide,   d. moon,   e. water
3. Sketches will vary.
4. Venus is close to the sun. It reflects most of the sunlight and looks like a bright star.
5. ©L©U D Y   A T M©S P H E R E   Circle the two C's and one O.
   Put them together for the chemical formula of carbon dioxide: CO_2.

ES-11. PLANET EARTH

1. a. (d),   b. (d),   c. (b),   d. (c),   e. (d),   f. (a),   g. (b),   h. (c),   i. (d),   j. (b)
2. mineral,   glacier,   rock,   trench,   weather
3. a. Because it's 80 percent rust: cRUST;   b. Because it has several FAULTS;
   c. Five letters: e, a, r, t, h;   d. The earth part;   e. It would be in the dark.

ES-12. PLANET MARS

1. a. image,   b. moons,   c. probes,   d. orbit,   e. Phobos,   f. lava,   g. Ares,
   h. polar;   *Bonus Item:* 4th.
2. valleys, dust, carbon dioxide, seasons, winds, polar caps
3. pink sky, no living organisms, rocks, water vapor

ES-13. PLANET JUPITER

1. a. hot material,   b. storm,   c. fifth,   d. twelve,   e. 90,   f. ball of gas,   g. 16,   h.
   Io, Europa
2. a . No (82,515),   b. Yes (87,100),   c. No (83,415)
3. 60
4. In the middle of the planet: "pit"

ES-14. PLANET SATURN

1. a. sixth,   b. second,   c. twenty,   d. colder,   e. division,   f. dense,   g. rings
2. ice,   rock,   sugar,   house
3. H = hydrogen,   He = helium, NH_3 = ammonia, CH_4 = methane

ES–15. PLANET URANUS

1. a. 8,   b. 9,   c. 2,   d. 11,   e. 7,   f. 4,   g. 5,   h. 3
2. hydrogen, methane, helium
3. "Uranus" (You ran us)
4. Line them up, one above the other, as you write their names. In this way they'll appear to be the same size.
5. ☀ = sun + U + a + r. Arrange the letters to spell Uranus.

ES–16. PLANET NEPTUNE

1. a. False: Neptune is the fourth largest planet;   b. True;   c. False: Neptune may be seen through a telescope;   d. True;   e. False: Neptune has a mean density of 1.7; f. False: Neptune has completed 0.92 or 92 percent of one orbit since its discovery; g. True;   h. False: Neptune has eight moons, and Triton, not Nereid, is the largest moon;   i. True;   j. False: Neptune refers to the Roman god of the sea.
2. frozen methane (CH_4)
3. The line over Point B should be 5.7 inches (14.5 cm) long.
4. <u>N</u> t <u>e</u> e p l t <u>e</u> u s <u>n</u> c <u>e</u> o p e

ES–17. PLANET PLUTO

Organisms *a, b, c, d, g, i,* and *k* should be found between Points 1 and 2; organisms *f* and *h* should be found between Points 2 and 3; organism *e* should be found between Points 3 and 4; organism *j* should be found between Points 4 and 1.

Pluto Puzzler: The two words separated by a line mean "god under world." Pluto was named after the god of the underworld.

ES–18. WE NEED THE WATER

1. molecule ocean fissure swamp creek horizon

    ellipse spring corona geyser craton pumice

    lake amber umbra river travertine aquifer a

    refraction dam regolith oxidation one ionc

    lave aquaduct epicenter glacier magnitude

2. Possible answers:

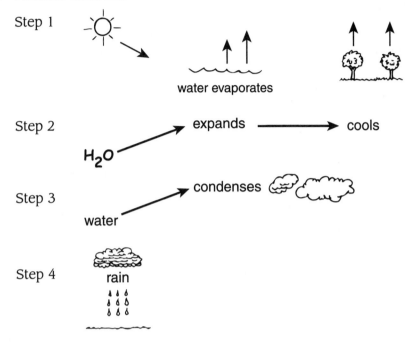

Step 1

water evaporates

Step 2

H_2O → expands ——→ cools

Step 3

water → condenses

Step 4

rain

ES–19. EARTH'S ATMOSPHERE

1. It will take 31 N's (78%) and 9 O's (21%).
2. Possible answers:
   A—air, argon, acid rain, aurora borealis
   T—troposphere, thunder, temperature, tornadoes
   M—meteors, mesosphere, monsoon, methane
   O—ozone layer, oxygen
   S—smoke, smog, snow, sleet, stratosphere, storms
   P—precipitation, pressure, pollution
   H—hydrogen, helium, heat, hail, hurricanes
   E—energy, elements
   R—rain, rays (light beams), radiation
   E—exosphere, electricity, evaporation
3. a. 1, 4,   b. 2, 3,   c. 1, 2,   d. 1, 3

ES–20. WEATHER INSTRUMENTS CODED NUMBERS

1. psychrometer,   2. barometer,   3. thermometer,   4. anemometer,   5. altimeter,
6. mercurial,   7. thermograph,   8. hygrometer,   9. barograph,   10. rain gauge

Secret Message: Rain, snow, hail, and sleet are forms of precipitation.

Weather Whizzer: They have two eyes: rain (i) and hail (i).

ES–21. AIR MASSES AND FRONTS

1. thousand of miles,   2. moisture and temperature,   3. place of origin,   4. holds much moisture,   5. cold and dry (either way),   6. warm and humid (either way),   7. to the ocean,   8. south gets warmer,   9. forms over land,   10. different air masses,   11. air masses collide,   12. produce violent weather,   13. does not move,   14. cold air mass,   15. in the weather,   16. a cold front,   17. and steady rain,   18. a cold front

ES–22. CLOUDS

1. A. Large area of water,   B. The sun's heat causes water to evaporate,   C. Water vapor rises into the atmosphere,   D. Air mass expands as it moves upward,   E. Moist air cools below its dew point,   F. Moist air condenses on dust particles,   G. Condensed water droplets form clouds

2. a. stratus,   b. cumulus,   c. cirrus

ES–23. TORNADOES AND HURRICANES

Correct statements (from top to bottom):

1. a. (144.12 divided by 6 = 24.02) A tornado may occur on a hot, humid day;   b. (2¼ divided by 3 = ¾) The air pressure of a tornado is much lower than normal atmospheric pressure;   c. (2½ + 3⅔ = 6⅙) Winds spinning within a tornado's funnel may reach 500 or more miles per hour.

2. a. warm moist air,   b. precipitation

ES–24. OCEAN SPEAK

A. 1. submersible, n;   2. sonar, j;   3. oceanographer, g;   4. continental, a;   5. submarine, b or i;   6. trench, o;   7. abyss, d;   8. marine, b or i;   9. saline, r;   10. guyot, c;   11. current, t;   12. diatom, h;   13. Cl-, f;   14. undertow, e;   15. thermocline, s;   16. sediment, k;   17. zooplankton, l;   18. shelf, m;   19. icebergs, p;   20. whitecap, q

B. *Sea Animal Puzzlers:*
    1. sand dollar,   2. sea star,   3. sea urchin,   4. plankton,   5. octopus

ES–25. SEA WATER

1. Mg + Cl, Ca + S, Na + Cl

2. a. INCREASES, Water evaporates. Solids are left behind;   b. DECREASES, Fresh water dilutes salt water;   c. INCREASES, Water evaporates. Solids are left behind;   d. DECREASES, Fresh water dilutes salt water;   e. DECREASES, Melting glaciers dilute salt water.

3. *Salty Puzzler:* Salinity = 3.8 percent (divide 2500 by 95). This is above-average salinity. Circle NO. A high salinity reading may indicate a hot, dry area where much evaporation takes place.

ES-26. PLANKTON IN THE SEA

1. perch, whale, albacore, sardine, mackeral, tuna, anchovy, herring
2. a. shark moving through water; b. plankton present in water; c. open mouth serves as a collecting unit; d. plankton pass through mouth; e. water filtered through gills and strained for food; f. shark swallows trapped plankton; g. plankton enters shark's stomach; h. plankton dinner nourishes shark

ES-27. SEA LIFE: PELAGIC ZONE

1. a. The shaded letters spell whale, squid, tuna, anchovy, rays, shark.
   b. The unshaded letters from top to bottom, left to right are: e, o, s, p, d, o, c, p; combined they spell copepods
2. a. dogfish, b. jellyfish, c. whale, d. squid, e. albacore, f. barracuda, g. seal.
3. The herring ends up inside the albacore (a **h l e** b r a r c i o n **r g** e).

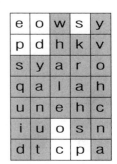

ES-28. SEA LIFE: BOTTOM DWELLERS

1. These organisms should be circled: (top row) albalone, chiton; (*middle row*) sea anemone, oysters; (*bottom row*) snails, mussel
2. 1. e, f; 2. a, f; 3. d, f; 4. b, f; 5. d, f; 6. d, f; 7. c, f
3. *Benthos Puzzler:* His last name is Crab. His full name is Neal Crab.

ES-29. SEA MAMMALS, PART 1

ACROSS: 2. warm, 4. rookery, 5. bulls, 8. echolocation, 9. dugong, 10. manatee
DOWN: 1. calves, 3. cows, 5. baleen, 6. otter, 7. dolphin

ES-30. SEA MAMMALS, PART 2

1. Question A: blubber; Question B: teeth

t	r	e	b	v	b	u	r	o	r	e	l	c	u	e	r	o	b	k	u	d
n	d	u	w	g	r	s	m	h	u	d	l	t	j	l	a	j	l	o	e	t
g	p	r	z	d	u	b	t	c	u	e	i	m	h	e	p	f	u	e	l	s
s	f	b	k	w	b	a	q	z	r	p	j	i	m	l	o	k	e	t	r	w
y	x	l	v	h	l	e	e	a	e	b	r	d	t	u	g	p	e	a	b	c

2. Question C: urchin; Question D: kelp; Question E: tests

i	h	c	k	n	i	u	e	c
	l	h	u	i	p	r	t	u	e
	n	s	h	n	t	c	r	s	r

3. pinniped

ES–31. TSUNAMI

1. Students should draw a wave about 2 inches (5 cm) high.
2. Read from bottom right to top left: third planet from the sun (earth) quake = earthquake.
3. Possible answers:
   T—trees, turtles, tarantulas
   S—snakes, snails, spiders, shrubs, sheep, sailors
   U—ungulates (hoofed animals), univalves (single-shell mollusks), urchins
   N—nematodes, newts
   A—amphibians, animals, arachnids, arthropods
   M—mammals, man, mice, marsupials, monkeys
   I—invertebrates, insects, iguanas

ES–32. PHYSICAL WEATHERING

1. wind, water, heat, frost
2. All three: The dots (A), dots and lines (B), and dots and crooked lines (C) suggest loose rock particles that may crumble easily.
3. The sixth vertical line from the left: *root*
4. Sketches will vary. Sketches should show cracked, broken rock particles.

ES–33. CHEMICAL WEATHERING

1. a. The part undergoing rust. The rusting process weakens the rock;
   b. It covers only the part where iron particles and oxygen combine.
2. Students should show Rock A crumbling and falling apart; the last sketch may reveal a small heap of rock particles.
3. carbon dioxide molecules—three;   water molecules—four
4. *Brain Dissolver:* six carbon, three hydrogen, and one oxygen

ES–34. GETTING INTO THE SOIL

1. Three centuries = 300 years; nine inches equal three centuries. Therefore, it would take about 550 years for 17 inches of soil to form.
2. bedrock, mantle rock, clay, silt
3. PED+AL (aluminum)+FE (iron) + R = Pedalfer soil. Al is the chemical symbol for aluminum and Fe is the chemical symbol for iron.
4. Yes. Oil is always found in soil (sOIL).

ES–35. THREE-WORD CLUE EROSION PUZZLE

1. running water;   2. soil erosion;   3. topsoil;   4. dust storm;   5. gravity;   6. peneplain;
7. high plateau;   8. runoff;   9. glacial ice;   10. creep;   11. mesa;   12. wind

ES–36. FUN WITH WATER

1. A. water table, B. waterfall, C. watershed
2. *Hydrogen* and *oxygen* combine *chemically* to form the *compound* water.
3. well, rapids, steam, ice, spring
4. a. Two molecules of water (There are 4 H's and 5 O's. This is enough to make two molecules of water.);   b. Two molecules of water (There are enough hydrogen and oxygen atoms to make two molecules of water.)

ES–37. ICE AGE

1. freeze, time, water, oxygen, temperature, hydrogen (Oxygen and hydrogen, of course, make up water.)
2. warming climate
3. Students can darken any part of the figure. They should shade in about 30 percent of the total area.
4. *Frosty Riddle:* Icesheets.

ES–38. GLACIERS

1. gravity, flow
2. crevasses
3. Possible answer: By its massive size and weight.
4. erode (Use the shape of the sign as the letter o to complete the spelling of erode.)
5. *Brain Boggler:* 3.6 miles

ES–39. MINERALS

1. a. sulfur, b. graphite, c. rutile, d. bauxite, e. serpentine, f. barite, g. muscovite, h. cuprite, i. azurite, j. fluorite, k. rhodonite, l. orthoclase, m. cassiterite, n. turquoise, o. corundum, p. tourmaline, q. chert
2. *Brain Buzzer:* iron
3. *Double Brain Buzzer:* mine

ES–40. GEMSTONES

1. opal, pearl, emerald, citrine, diamond, topaz, ruby, sapphire
2. size, flaws, color, luster, hardness, crystal
3. gem, gem, gem, garnet, opal
4. *Bonus Puzzler:* GEMstone

ES–41. ROCK TALK

1. Diagram B. Rearrange the first letter in each mineral name to produce a ROCK.

2. Diagram A. It has the letters that spell MINERALS, the makeup of rocks. Diagrams B and C show only partial letters in the spelling of minerals.

3. Diagram B. It contains the letters needed to spell QUARRY, excavation of rocks. This would be the best producer of rocks.

ES–42. IGNEOUS INTRUSION

1. Diagrams will vary. Figure A should show coarse-grained particles mixed with large crystals. Figure B should show fine-grained particles with small crystals or no crystals present.

2. a. intrusive,   b. extrusive,   c. extrusive,   d. extrusive

3. Granite: 1, 6, 3; Basalt: 4, 2, 5

ES–43. MIGHTY METAMORPHIC

1. ACROSS: 2. shale, 3. limestone, 4. granite, 5. schist

   DOWN: 1. sandstone, 4. gneiss

2. Sketches will vary. The fossilized fish should be unrecognizable.

ES–44. SEDIMENTARY INQUIRY

1. 1. g,   2. d,   3. c,   4. h,   5. f,   6. b,   7. a,   8. e

2. a. conglomerate, b. siltstone, c. chalk, d. limestone, e. shale, f. coal, g. sandstone

ES–45. DIASTROPHISM

1. The connected dots should show land rising above the surrounding area; a. heat, pressure, and internal forces in the earth's crust; b. mountains, hills, and terraces

2. The connected dots should show a sinking of land below the surrounding area; a. added weight of sediment, increased gravity in these areas. Internal forces, heat, and pressure causing earthquakes and volcanic eruptions may cause certain areas of the floor to sink;   b. basins, sea floors, and valley floors

3. Students should darken two areas in the right half of the box. Arrows would indicate horizontal movement; heat, pressure, and internal forces in the earth's crust.

ES-46. MOUNTAINS AND HILLS

1. MOUNTAINS: a, b, c, d, g, h, j, k, l, m, n, o, p, q;
   HILLS: b, c, e, f, i, k, l, m, p;
   a. Definitions will vary.
   b. Definitions will vary.

2. Possible profiles:

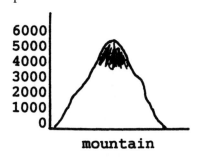 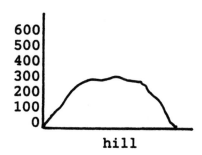

ES-47. MOVING CONTINENTS

Possible answers:

1. (Part 1) A—alluvial fan, atoll; L—levee, laccolith, lagoon, landslide, lake;
   F—fault, fiord, fissure; R—river, ridge; E—extrusive rock, extinct volcano; D—dam,
   diastrophism, desert, delta, dune, drumlin; W—well, waterfall, weather, wind; E—
   element, exfoliation, esker; G—granite, guyot, gully, glacier, gorge; E—escarpment,
   entrenched meander; N—Névé, neck (volcanic), natural levee, Niagara Falls;
   E—estuary, erosion, earthquake; R—reservoir, rapids, rocks

   (Part 2) P—pyroxene, plagioclase feldspar, pyrite, pitchblende; A—agate, aragonite,
   azurite; N—nephelite, nemalite, natrolite, noble opal; G—graphite, galena, garnet,
   gypsum, gabbro; A—apatite, anorthite, anhydrite; E—epidote, emerald, embolite,
   enstatite; A—amethyst, anglesite, aquamarine, amblygonite

2. He lost the mineral apatite. Therefore, he must have suffered from a loss of "apatite."

3. plate tectonics

ES-48. LANDFORMS

1. mountains and plains (The letters spelling plains are inside the letters spelling
   mountains: m o <u>p</u> l u n <u>a</u> i t a <u>n</u> <u>s</u> i n s.)

2. Possible answers:
   a. erosional and weathering forces: water, wind, mechanical and chemical
      weathering, perhaps glaciation, faulting, etc.
   b. erosional and weathering forces: water, wind, mechanical and chemical
      weathering
   c. accumulation of sand due to wind deposits
   d. mountain building may involve folding, faulting, uplift, volcanic action, and so on

3. *Landform Puzzler:* valley, beach

ES–49. VOLCANIC MAGIC

1. a. Magma may be described as hot liquid rock mass.   b. "The atmosphere?"
2. gases, lava, steam, fragments, dust, sulfur dioxide, ash, explosion
3. Shield: piece 1 (⌒); Cinder: pieces 4 and 2 (⌃);
   Composite: pieces 3, 5, and 6 (⌣)
4. *Red Hot Riddle:* a spent vent

ES–50. VOLCANIC ATTACK

1. tephra,   2. obsidian,   3. fissure,   4. pumice,   5. magma,   6. water vapor,
7. cinders,   8. crater,   9. basalt,   10. carbon dioxide,   11. cone,   12. explosive,
13. oozing,   14. active,   15. dormant,   16. extinct,   17. composite,   18. caldera,
19. scoria,   20. shield

Mystery Question: STRATO-volcano.

ES–51. EARTHQUAKE LINGO

Richter, S wave, stress, fault, aftershock, quake, focus, fracture, kinetic, tremor, San Andreas, P wave, seismic, magnitude, energy, epicenter

Earthquake Riddles: 1. "Don't blame me. It's not my fault."   2. No-Fault

ES–52. FOSSILS

1. a. frog (PF),   b. seed (PF),   c. rock (NW),   d. soil (NW),   e. fern (PF),   f. clay (NW),
   g. skin (PF),   h. bird (PF),   i. iron (NW),   j. fish (PF)
2. abdomen, antennae, walking legs, thorax
3. (*circled*) horsetail, diatoms, lepidodendron;
   (*underlined*) sea lily, mollusk, pecten (scallop)
4. Flossi would have to switch the l and i in her name. Then she would become a Fossil, the preserved remains of an ancient organism.
5. She used the letters in her name to spell dinosaur.
6. one foot (or 12 inches or 30.48 centimeters)
7. animal fossil
8. Saying its name

ES–53. PREHISTORIC ORGANISMS

a. 5,   b. 4,   c. 1,   d. 2,   e. 3,   f. 18,   g. 17,   h. 11,   i. 12,   j. 7,   k. 6,
l. 10,   m. 8,   n. 9,   o. 15,   p. 13,   q. 16,   r. 14

Brain Pain: Who knows? Perhaps something "paranoid."

ES–54. PRECAMBRIAN ERA

1. The letters in the advertisement may be used to spell era, periods, and epochs
2. Sketches will vary. Sketches should show evidence of twisting, tearing, and stretching—forces exerted during metamorphism.
3. algae, graphite, fossils, jellyfish
4. Life can be found in the Precambrian: prleciamfbreian.

ES–55. PALEOZOIC ERA

1. a. coral   b. reef   c. warm   d. adapt   e. giant
   f. fish   g. snail   h. clams   i. algae   j. shark
   The darkened boxes describe a large body of salt water known as a sea.
2. CLUE: algae. The letters that spell the name of each critter are mixed with the letters that spell algae: a. sponge,   b. mollusk,   c. fish,   d. jellyfish

ES–56. MESOZOIC ERA

1. dinosaurs, birds, mammals, gastropods (snails), pelecypods (clams, etc.), conifers (cone-bearing plants), ferns (All names have a vowel for the second letter.)
2. plants, meat
3. disease, climatic, mammals, impact
4. *Mesozoic Riddle:* the letter s

ES–57. CENOZOIC ERA

1. PLANTS: cypress, grasses, palms, sequoias;   INVERTEBRATES: insects, mussels, spiders, starfish;   VERTEBRATES: amphibians, lemurs, mammoths, reptiles
2. woolly mammoth, mastodon
3. *Cenozoic Riddle:* the ant part: elephANT

Life Science

LS–1. LIFE

1. ACROSS: 7. photosynthesis
   DOWN: 1. adapt,   2. response,   3. stimulus,   4. energy,   5. develop,   6. life span
2. multicellular
3. a. appearance,   b. triumphant,   c. clasp,   d. trampoline,   e. femur,   f. share,
   g. clamp,   h. ticket,   i. scratcher,   j. cashew,   k. signature,   l. dynamite,
   m. street,   n. configure,   o. supine,   p. scooter,   q. blouse,   r. confiscate

LS–2. CELLS, PART 1

1. a. bacterium, blood, paramecium, nerve; b. jellyfish, tapeworm, ant, mosquito
2. 1. e,   2. d,   3. a,   4. c,   5. b
3. a. osmosis, b. mitosis, c. tissue, d. membrane, e. nucleus, f. centriole, g. ribosome

LS–3. CELLS, PART 2

(*Possible Answers*)
1. a. *Plant Cell:* Plant cells are box-shaped, not long and narrow; the cytoplasm is inside the cell, not where the cell wall would be. The nucleolus is inside the nucleus. The line is touching the nucleus. Chlorophyll should be inside the chloroplast, not scattered within the cytoplasm. The plant cell does not have centrioles.
     b. *Animal Cell:* Animal cells are round-shaped, not box-like. The animal cell does not have a cell wall. The animal cell does not have chloroplasts.
2. Cell can be spelled a total of four times. The sides of the container may be used as two letter l's.

LS–4. CELL DIVISION

INTERPHASE: resting cell; not dividing.   PROPHASE: chromosomes appear.
METAPHASE: chromosome pairs line up.   ANAPHASE: chromosomes split apart.
TELOPHASE: two cells form.

LS–5. VIRUSES

1. a, d, and e are true
2. polio, rabies, mumps, measles, german measles, AIDS
3. nucleic acid + protein coat
4. To see viruses, they'd have to be under magnification, not UNDER the microscope.
5. Both remain at rest until activated.

LS–6. MONERANS, PART 1

1. a. circle oxygen: nitrogen,   b. circle animals: organisms,   c. circle can: cannot (*exception:* cyanobacteria make their own food), d. circle spirillum: bacillus, e. circle harmful: harmless,   f. circle some: all,   g. circle nuclear: binary, h. circle bacteria: viruses
2. a. cheese,   b. butter,   c. yogurt; *Bonus Question:* toxins
3. a. bacteria in the cafeteria,   b. a nitrogen—"fixation,"   c. the spreading of bacteria

LS–7. MONERANS, PART 2

1. a. fission,   b. saprophyte,   c. shape,   d. heterotroph,   e. tail
2. a. 5—pathogen,   b. 2—spirilla,   c. 6—organism,   d. 3—flagella,   e. 1—botulism, f. 4—bacillus

LS-8. PROTISTA

amoeba (sarcodine): 2, 5, 6, 7, 10, 11, 12, 18, 20, 21, 22;
paramecium (ciliate): 1, 3, 5, 6, 7, 11, 13, 14, 15, 16, 18, 19, 22, 23;
euglena (flagellate): 2, 4, 5, 6, 8, 9, 11, 12, 17, 18, 21, 22, 24, 25;
plasmodium (sporozoan): 2, 5, 6, 21, 22, 26, 27, 28

LS-9. FUNGI

1. a. make their own food,   b. chlorophyll
2. saprophyte
3. a. mold,   b. morel,   c. mildew,   d. rusts,   e. smuts,   f. yeasts
4. The letters in Mr. O Shumo spell mushroom, an edible fungus.
5. "pear" + "ah" + "sign" + t = parasite

LS-10. PLANTS, PART 1

1. Students need only draw thin lines along each branch from the pot to the end of the branch.
2. Once again, students draw thin lines from the branches into each leaf and stem.
3. poppy, fern, spruce, cedar, potato, gingko, cypress, rose

LS-11. PLANTS, PART 2

1. a. xylem,   b. monocot,   c. stomata,   d. pistil,   e. conifer,   f. fronds,
    g. gymnosperms,   h. seed,   i. phloem,   j. angiosperms,   k. petiole,   l. root,
    m. fruit,   n. sepals,   o. stamen,   p. cork
2. a. Rearrange the letter in its name from flea to leaf;   b. three different flower
    arrangements;   c. a square root;   d. a small yellowish-orange fruit;   e. a "rooting"
    section;   f. The letters p, e, a, l (sEPAL) make up 80 percent of PEtAL.

LS-12. PLANTS, PART 3

1. algae, cotton, fern, fir, grass, hemp, ivy, oak, rice, sycamore, wheat, yam
2. *(Possible Answers)* a. corn, beans, cucumbers, asparagus, any fruits;   b. palm, grass,
    bamboo;   c. grass skirt, straw hat;   d. many flower varieties, wood products;
    e. codeine (opium plants), quinine (tree bark), aloe vera (for cuts and burns);
    f. any green plant
3. a. "No, no. I" is onion   b. "rad is H" is radish   c. "bee, T" is beet
    d. "Let cute" is lettuce   e. "May" is yam   f. "OK, ra" is okra

LS–13. SIMPLE INVERTEBRATES: SPONGES

1. Sketches will vary. Students should include several holes or pores in their drawings.
2. a. water,   b. synthetic,   c. pores,   d. regenerate,   e. spicule,   f. spineless,
    g. sessile,   h. flagella,   i. asexual,   j. collar,   k. organs,   l. oscula
3. a. In the letter O: sp**O**nge, b. He was becoming too much of a sponge.

LS–14. SIMPLE INVERTEBRATES: CORALS AND SEA ANEMONES

1. ocean, polyp, reef, atoll, jewelry
2. polyp
3. tentacles, capture, stinging cells, poison
4. tentacles, soft-bodied, mouth, marine, central cavity, polyps

LS–15. SIMPLE INVERTEBRATES: HYDRAS AND JELLYFISH

1. false: b, c, e, f, h, j, m, p

    (*Explanations:* b. There is no sessile medusa stage;   c. Hydras do not have whip-like tail structures;   e. A medusa is a free-swimming cup-like form of a cnidarian; f. Hydras live in a fresh water environment;   h. Jellyfish do not have holes or pores lining their body;   j. Hydras have the ability to move from one place to another; m. The polyp is the asexual generation of a jellyfish;   p. Hydras reproduce by budding, an outgrowth of the parent organism)

2. Responses will vary. *Possible Answer:* "The jelly in jellyfish."
3. The three animals hiding in the puzzle are the sea anemone, coral, and jellyfish. The darkened spaces spell SEA: They live in the sea.

LS–16. WORMS

1. a. 1,2,4,8,9,15   b. 2,3,4,8,11,14   c. 2,3,4,6,7,11,13   d. 1,2,4,6,7,9,14
    e. 2,4,6,8,12,13   f. 2,4,5,6,8,12,15   g. 2,4,6,8,12,13   h. 1,2,4,8,9
    i. 2,4,6,7,10,12   j. 2,4,6,8,12   k. 2,3,4,7,11   l. 2,4,6,7,10

2. a. The <u>chin</u> is located under the lower lip: trichina;   b. An athletic trainer needs <u>tape</u>: tapeworm;   c. A <u>scar</u> is a sign of tissue damage: ascaris

LS–17. MORE WORMS

1. trichina worm,   2. leech,   3. sheep liver fluke,   4. tapeworm,   5. earthworm

LS-18. MOLLUSKS

1. slug, squid, chiton, limpet, abalone
2. Drawings will vary. Most should look like a typical garden snail.
3. Snail B would move its foot.
4. a. Aren't boys terrible? (oyster)
   b. Carol's luggage got lost at the airport. (slug)
   c. Bambi Valveoni is the best female athlete in school. (bivalve)
   d. Helen's nail got caught in her wood sweater. (snail)
   e. Mr. C. hit one ball from the tee to the green. (chiton)
5. a. auger, b. foot, c. shell

LS-19. ECHINODERMS

1. star, urchin, cucumber, dollar, lily
2. endoskeleton
3. a. ocean; b. radial; c. feet; d. tube, spines; e. replace; f. water
4. Because it "lies" on the bottom of the ocean.

LS-20. ARTHROPODS

1. gastropod, nautilus
2. exoskeleton
3. centipede
4. circulatory, head, bodies, thorax, molting, appendage

LS-21. ARTHROPODS: ARACHNIDS

1. ACROSS: 2. blood, 3. two, 5. mites, 6. simple, 8. spinnerets, 9. eight, 11. insects
   DOWN: 1. abdomen, 4. six pair, 7. desert, 10. ticks
2. a. under someone's shoe, b. between the letters p and d: spider

LS-22. ARTHROPODS: CRUSTACEANS

1. a. shell   b. gills
   c. regenerate d. jaws
   e. moist   f. claws
   g. barnacle   h. swimmerets
   i. carapace   j. krill
   k. two   l. antennae
   m. compound   n. five
2. The rust part: cRUSTacean.

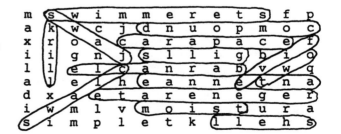

LS-23. ARTHROPODS: CENTIPEDES AND MILLIPEDES

1. Sketches will vary. *Key to drawing:* one pair of legs per body segment; flat body.
2. Sketches will vary. *Key to drawing:* two pairs of legs per body segment; round body.
3. The centipede likes to bite. *Clues:* "lip"—mil<u>LIP</u>ede; "tip"—cent<u>ip</u>ede.

LS-24. ARTHROPODS: INSECTS

1.

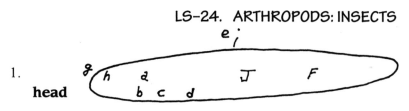

2. chiton, sow bug, pillbug
3. one; bee *or* beetle (It doesn't say you can use a letter more than once.)

LS-25. ARTHROPODS: MORE INSECTS

1. head, thorax, abdomen
2. a. termite,   b. butterfly,   c. mosquito,   d. bed bug,   e. cicada,   f. ladybug
3. 5 bristletails (The other organisms aren't insects!)
4. grounded
5. The "tic" of the tick replaced the "cric" of the cricket. Together they formed a "ticket" and used it to get in and see the show.

LS-26. VERTEBRATES

1. tuna,   2. viper,   3. pigeon,   4. squirrel,   5. mammoth,   6. shrew,   7. robin,
8. osprey,   9. manatee,   10. tortoise,   11. sturgeon,   12. rhino,   13. salmon,
14. bison,   15. albacore,   16. hyena,   17. perch,   18. gorilla,   19. vulture,   20. pike,
21. porcupine,   22. raccoon,   23. hare,   24. woodpecker

Vertebrate Puzzler: (Possible Answers) beaver, rat, bat, bear

LS-27. VERTEBRATES: FISH, PART 1

1.

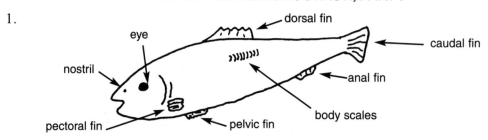

2. a. 3;   b. 4;   c. 8;   d. 1;   e. 5, 7;   f. 5, 7;   g. 5, 7;   h. 5, 7;   i. 6
3. a. 2;   b. 10

LS–28. VERTEBRATES: FISH, PART 2

1. flexible cartilage
2. fins
3. $\dfrac{\text{humans}}{\text{fish}}$ (humans overfish)
4. Man-eating tuna sandwich (man-eating fish).
5. It's possible if the sea perch is a pregnant female.
6. She could tell by the "scales" on its tail.

LS–29. VERTEBRATES: AMPHIBIANS

1. a. cave salamander,   b. mudpuppy,   c. tree frog,   d. toad
2. caecilian, hellbender, toad, siren, tadpole, leopard frog, newt, axolotl
3. Turn "HOH" into H_2O (water).
4. a. An insect eaten tail first by a salamander.
   b. Hibernate *through* the winter (amphibians do this).

LS–30. VERTEBRATES: REPTILES

1. a. gila monster,   b. tortoise,   c. python;   *Bonus Item:* taipan
2. a. legless tree snake (Snakes do not have legs.);   b. three or four-chambered heart;
   c. cold-blooded vertebrates;   d. head of an alligator;   e. dry, tropical climates;
   f. on land
3. a. Because ALL young reptiles look EXACTLY like their parents;   b. captivity;
   c. in the animal classification system
4. skink (SKINk)

LS–31. VERTEBRATES: BIRDS

1. toothless, lightweight
2. five: four claws, one talon
3. sexually, backbone
4. a. roach,   b. caiman,   c. mudskipper
5. a. All of the feathers on a bird is known as plummage. The letters in his name spell
   plummage;   b. b-i-r-d
6. a. some birds fly lower because they have more DOWN feathers;   b. Santa "claws"

LS–32. VERTEBRATES: MAMMALS, PART 1

1. a. 2, b. 7, c. 4, d. 20, e. 14, f. 15, g. 18, h. 8, i. 3, j. 21, k. 16, l. 12,
   m. 22, n. 6, o. 19, p. 5, q. 23, r. 10, s. 17, t. 9, u. 13, v. 11, w. 1
2. a. A "bison"tennial,   b. He got tired of the kids calling him "Bobcat,"
   c. Hu"manatee" (humanity)

LS-33. VERTEBRATES: MAMMALS, PART 2

1. a. warm-blooded, b. four-chambered heart, c. body hair, d. intelligence, e. mammary glands
2. llama
3. pattern
4. a. Manx cat, b. marmoset, c. moose, d. muskrat, e. manatee, f. mammoth, g. mongoose

LS-34. HUMAN SKELETAL SYSTEM, PART 1

1. a. tibia, radius, patella, cranium, lumbar, fibula, scapula
   b. humerus, ischium
   c. ilium
2. pivotal, hinge, gliding, socket

LS-35. HUMAN SKELETAL SYSTEM, PART 2

1. 22
2. 206
3. tralschy oidmtar salrit paul nate
   brnasa lowxyg tmber vico ccyx
   stern thorac risac rumc foli
4. femur, sternum, scapula, clavicle; *Bonus Item:* ear
5. *Bone Riddles:* a. "fore"arm bones, b. radius

LS-36. HUMAN MUSCLE SYSTEM, PART 1

ACROSS: 2. skeletal, 3. stomach, 6. tendon, 9. contraction, 10. involuntary
DOWN: 1. pairs, 4. cardiac, 5. flexor, 7. voluntary, 8. extensor

Muscle Riddle: "me" (muscle)

LS-37. HUMAN MUSCLE SYSTEM, PART 2

1.
a. hamstring   d. cardiac
b. masseter   e. bicep
c. sternomastoid   f. deltoid

2. *Tissue Puzzler:* connective tissue

LS-38. HUMAN DIGESTIVE SYSTEM

1. bolus (bo+lus),   chyme (chy+me),   esophagus (es+oph+ag+us),
   glands (gla+nds),   mucus (mu+cus),   stomach (sto+ma+ch),
   taste (ta+ste),   teeth (tee+th)

2.

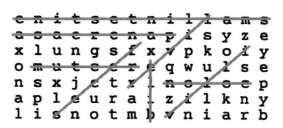

   bile,   colon,   feces,   liver,   pancreas,   rectum,   small intestine,   villi

LS-39. HUMAN CIRCULATORY SYSTEM

1. a. arteries,   b. vascular,   c. atrium,   d. ventricle,   e. pulmonary,   f. aorta,
   g. veins,   h. capillaries,   i. heart,   j. valves,   k. plasma
2. a. blood to veins to right atrium to right ventricle to pulmonary artery to
   pulmonary artery branches to lungs;   b. oxygen, carbon dioxide
3. left atrium, left ventricle, aorta, aorta, arteries

LS-40. HUMAN RESPIRATORY SYSTEM

1. nitrogen;   2. cilia;   3. respiration;   4. nostrils;   5. trachea;   6. bronchi;
7. alveoli, oxygen, carbon dioxide;   8. alveolus;   9. respiratory system;
10. epiglottis;   11. inflate;   12. deflate;   13. breathe;   14. diaphragm;
15. inspiration;   16. capillaries

Bonus Puzzler: pneu + mo + nia = pneumonia

LS-41. HUMAN EXCRETORY SYSTEM

1. a. urine, bladder;   b. water, salts, ureter;   *Bonus Question:* urethra
2. sweat glands

LS-42. HUMAN NERVOUS SYSTEM

1. pain   2. impulse   3. motor   4. stimulus   5. skin
6. axon   7. neuron   8. dendrite   9. reflex   10. ganglia
11. cerebellum   12. synapse   13. cerebrum   14. meninges   15. brain

Bonus Problem: 1.85 (divide 162 into 3)

LS-43. HUMAN SENSORY SYSTEM

1. taste	2. sound	3. receptors	4. eye	5. sensation
6. tactile	7. olfactory	8. stimuli	9. buds	10. skin
11. anesthetic	12. tongue	13. bitter	14. messages	15. iris
16. ear	17. flavor			

Bonus Question: retina

LS-44. HUMAN ENDOCRINE SYSTEM

1. gonad, adrenal, ovary, pineal, thyroid, thymus
2. a. kidney; b. brain; c. neck; d. stomach; e. pelvic area, male
3. adrenals, adrenaline, prepares body for stress; pituitary, body growth hormone, controls growth and other glands; pancreas, insulin, regulates blood–sugar levels; testes, testosterone, controls/regulates male organs; thyroid, thyroxin, controls rate of metabolism; ovaries, estrogen, controls/regulates female organs

Thought Provoker: bloodstream

LS-45. HUMAN REPRODUCTIVE SYSTEM

1. genetic; 2. penis; 3. semen; 4. ovaries; 5. oviduct; 6. oviduct; 7. vagina;
8. menstrual; 9. conception; 10. uterus; 11. zygote; 12. chromosomes;
13. larger; 14. testes; 15. estrogen; 16. testosterone; 17. fallopian; 18. uterus;
19. amniotic; 20. ovulation; 21. umbilical cord, placenta; 22. placenta; 23. fetus;
24. gestation; 25. amnion

LS-46. INFECTIOUS DISEASES

1. Pathogen, 2. Infection, 3. Salmonella, 4. immunization, 5. histoplasmosis,
6. bacteria, 7. antibiotic, 8. vaccination, 9. disinfectant, 10. transmit,
11. communicable, 12. protist, 13. mononucleosis, 14. chicken pox, 15. scarlet fever

Bonus Try: bacteria, spreading

LS-47. CHRONIC DISORDERS

1. 1,12,22; 2,11,23; 3,15,18; 4,14,19; 5,13,21; 6,9,20; 7,10,24; 8,16,17
2. bronchitis, allergy, cancer, sinusitis, hepatitis, asthma, arthritis, diabetes

LS-48. USE OF DRUGS

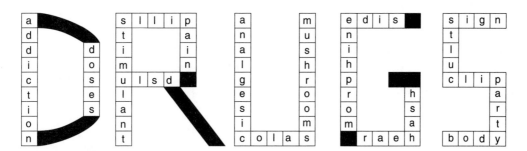

1. addiction, 2. stimulant, 3. pills, 4. pain, 5. LSD, 6. analgesic, 7. colas, 8. doses, 9. mushrooms, 10. morphine, 11. side, 12. hash, 13. hear, 14. sign, 15. cults, 16. clip, 17. party, 18. body

LS-49. USE OF ALCOHOL

1. escape, 2. less, 3. depress, 4. bloodstream, 5. nervous, 6. hallucinations, 7. most, 8. decreases, 9. detoxification, 10. cirrhosis, 11. tolerance, 12. alcoholism, 13. stomach, 14. enlarge, 15. fermented, 16. physically, 17. liquor, 18. reaction, 19. heat, 20. metabolized

LS-50. USE OF TOBACCO, PART 1

1. arsenic, 2. women, 3. larynx, 4. carton, 5. alveoli, 6. bronchitis, 7. emphysema, 8. mucus, 9. lesion, 10. cancer, 11. snuff, 12. chew, 13. cough, 14. nicotine, 15. smoking, 16. habit

Mystery Question: carcinogen

LS-51. USE OF TOBACCO, PART 2

1. dermis, throat, tongue, arteries, tissue, gums, esophagus, smoke, trachea
2. bad, smelly, smoke
3. Answers to response items will vary. Here are some possible responses:
   a. No, it's never too late. The moment Marvin stops smoking, he'll cease pouring chemicals into his body.
   b. Probably not. The rising cost of cigarettes does little to combat addiction to tobacco use.
   c. Mary and Don have the right to set rules in their home. This is not a rude behavior. Mary and Don share a concern for a healthy lifestyle.

LS–52. HEREDITY, PART 1

A. 36+ percent of students. No. The class sample is too small.
B. Descriptions will vary.
C. 1. The nucleus controls cellular activities.
    2. Chromosomes in the nucleus of a cell control heredity.
    3. Genes are found on chromosomes.
    4. Genes control all the traits of an organism.
D. *Just for Fun:* 8

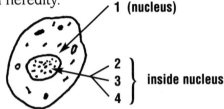

LS–53. HEREDITY, PART 2

A. Possible answer: DNA contains all the information needed to be passed from parents to offspring.
B. 1. eye or eyeball,   2. ear,   3. brain,   4. bone,   5. blood,   6. cell,   7. neuron
C. Sketches will vary.
    A simple sketch may look like this:
D. An organism with numerous genes will, in turn, show a variety of traits. Thus, there would be different organisms with many different traits.

LS–54. HEREDITY, PART 3

A. gene
    trait
    code
    cross
    gamete

B. tall
    short
    smooth
    wrinkled

C.

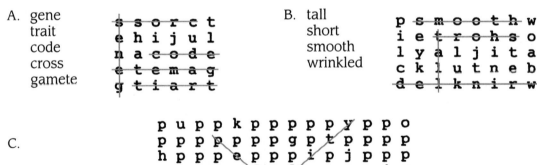

pure, probability, pedigree, phenotype

LS-55. EVOLUTION, PART 1

1. earlier, nonliving, generation
2. slow, difficult, experimentally
3. selection, fittest
4. did (or believed), *The Origin of Species*
5. inherited, evolutionary
6. aren't, offspring
7. variation, different form

LS-56. EVOLUTION, PART 2

A. (*Possible Answers*) earthquakes, volcanoes, mountain-building processes, erosion, weathering, landslides

B. Any organisms alive today have adapted to changing environmental conditions. *Examples:*

A—ant, antelope, anteater, angiosperm, etc.

D—dog, dandelion, duck, donkey, etc.

A—alligator, amphibians, arthropoda, etc.

P—porpoise, penguin, palm tree, Porifera, etc.

T—tortoise, tiger, tuna, termite, etc.

C. a. trait   b. variations   c. population   d. fossils   e. finch   f. gradualism
g. extinction   h. Lamarck   i. Darwin   j. Beagle

D. *Evolution Problem:* $\dfrac{\text{change}}{\text{time}}$ (change over time)

LS-57. ECOLOGY, PART 1

1. niche (second row)
2. interact (first row)
3. community (second row)
4. producer (second row)
5. decomposer (second row)
6. consumer (first row)
7. biome (first row)
8. habitat (second row)

LS-58. ECOLOGY, PART 2

1. sunshine, temperatures, rich, ample
2. a. sun to weeds to mouse to snake to owl
   b. diatoms to large protozoans to small crustaceans to giant water bugs to fish to herons
3. (*True Statements*) c, e, i, m

Bonus Problem: mice

Physical Science

PS–1. PHYSICAL SCIENCE PUZZLE

1. compound, heat, energy, base, oxidize, physical, refraction, molecule, mass, electricity, kinetic, chemical, sound, acid, matter, suspension, spectrum, ionize, zinc, alloy, power
2. a. Mostly in three states: solid, liquid and gas
   b. As a hammer drives a nail into the wooden board, the head of a nail warms.

PS–2. M AND S TERMS

1. a. matter, b. solute, c. solid, d. mass, e. solar, f. speed, g. magma, h. meter, i. metal, j. malleable, k. symbols, l. sound, m. miscible, n. milli, o. methane, p. salt, q. silica, r. momentum, s. machine, t. suspension
2. a. electrolytes, b. element, c. erg

PS–3. PHYSICAL SCIENTISTS

A. 1. d ("end"),   2. f ("oro"),   3. h ("ant" and "hen"),   4. g. ("Roe"),   5. a ("rie" and "rie"),   6. e ("Newt"),   7. b ("hi"–"hi"),   8. c ("ann" or "anne")
B. *Object:* sodium atom; *Statement:* The eight dots and numbers two and one represent electrons. The sodium atom has 11 electrons, negatively (–) charged.

PS–4. PROBLEM SOLVING

1. 7 d's—1970s

2. All of them: The ╫╫╫╫╫ represents a symbol for railroad track or line. Plumber and engineer would be lines of work.

3. ▅▅▅ = Ⅷ, ∞ = 8, {⧈} the vertical circles touch for an eight, three eights are formed from ⬦. Therefore, there are seven eights.

4. Three: snail, man, and animals

5. 4 + Ⅳ = eight or ⅠⅠⅠⅠ + ⅠⅠⅠⅠ = eight

6. Two: ⌞ + ⌐ = ▯

7. The moon going through various phases: → →

8. Write the word "friction" on a piece of paper. Then erase it. You've used friction between the eraser and paper to eliminate the word "friction."

PS–5. SCIENTIFIC LAWS

1. Law of Conservation of Matter
2. Law of Definite Proportions
3. Law of Universal Gravitation
4. Law of Conservation of Energy
5. Pascal's Law
6. Boyle's Law
7. Law of Conservation of Momentum
8. Newton's First Law of Motion

Message: A scientific law will *predict* the *results* of a given situation.

PS–6. MEASUREMENT

1. a. 10.97 cubits,   b. 205.7 cubits,   c. 14.4 cubits,   d. 31.5 cubits
2. a. 6,106 grams, 61.1 kilograms;   b. 76.2 cm;   c. 1,825 liters;   d. 1,679.8 grams;
   e. Sarah weighs 5.2 pounds more than Christina.
3. a. 5,   b. 3,   c. 4,   d. 1,   e. 2
4. (*Possible answers*)
   a. As long as you wish
   b. As high as it is, any height, as high as you wish, way above ground

PS–7. METRIC SYSTEM

1. a. centi,   b. gram,   c. liter,   d. meter,   e. kilometer,   f. millimeters,   g. milliliter,
   h. kilogram,   i. milli,   j. meter,   k. kilo,   l. liter,   m. centigram,   n. newton,
   o. centimeters,   p. meter
2. a metric "ruler"
3. Meter + Liter = ME+LI. Unscramble the letters to spell MILE.

PS–8. A LOOK AT ALCHEMY

1. Answers will vary. (*Possible responses*) become a compulsive gambler; allow drugs to control your life; spend more money than you earn; continue to make poor investments; lead a life of crime
2. Answers will vary. (*Possible responses*) lie about their age; spend large amounts of money on cosmetic surgery; consume large quantities of vitamins and minerals; get plenty of sleep; eat nutritious foods, and do regular exercise; wear "young looking" clothes; keep company with young people; keep a youthful attitude
3. Answers will vary. The wildest imaginations, of course, will produce the most bizarre recipes.

PS-9. INTRODUCING MATTER, PART 1

1. (*Possible answers*) rat, tar, mat, meat, tea, tee, arm, tram, ram, mare
2. a. 83.3 grams, b. 3.83 pounds, c. 83 pounds, d. 88 kilograms,
    e. they all have number 8 in the answer.
3. a. | mat - ter |

    b. Each number equals the letter number as it appears in the English alphabet:
    a = 1, b = 2, etc. Convert all numbers to letters, unscramble the letters, and
    spell MATTER.
4. mass destruction

PS-10. INTRODUCING MATTER, PART 2

1. metal, 2. alkali, 3. temperature, 4. tin, 5. evaporate, 6. rust, 7. oxygen,
8. fusion, 9. liquid, 10. alloy, 11. weight, 12. compound, 13. oil, 14. neutron,
15. solvent, 16. energy, 17. reaction, 18. viscous, 19. atom, 20. thermal,
21. ion, 22. ores, 23. nitrogen, 24. oxidation, 25. fission
Bonus Challenge: Law of Conservation of Matter

PS-11. MATTER PUZZLERS

1. Combine w with 8 for *weight*; combine s + p + ace for *space*.
2. a. gas, b. bird, c. ring, d. compass, e. plant, f. hydrogen, g. pyramid,
    h. water, i. helium, j. steam
3. iron, zinc, tin, No (Nobelium), K (Potassium), potassium, Fe (Iron), lead, Pb (Lead),
    At (Astatine), silicon
4. salad, food, concrete (dried mixed materials), succotash (lima beans and corn),
    soil (mixture of dirt and humus)
5. Comlb. Lb is an abbreviation for pound.

PS-12. STATE OF MATTER: SOLID

A. 1. phase, 2. wood, 3. plastic, 4. brick, 5. conduction, 6. mass, 7. property,
    8. glass, 9. density, 10. molecules, 11. rock, 12. freezing, 13. volume,
    14. shape, 15. particles, 16. crystals, 17. ice, 18. copper
B. *Puzzler #1:* the sol part—Sol refers to sun, our closest gaseous star
    Puzzler #2: the lid (movable box cover)

PS-13. STATE OF MATTER: LIQUID

A. *Across:* 2. soup, 4. tea, 5. steam, 7. condensation, 9. sweat, 10. milk;
    Down: 1. vapor, 2. soda, 3. rain, 6. evaporation, 7. coffee, 8. dew
B. 1. soup, 2. sweat, 3. milk, 4. soda, 5. evaporation, 6. tea

PS-14. STATE OF MATTER: GAS

A. 1. Nitrogen,   2. Container,   3. Volume,   4. Argon,   5. Hydrogen,   6. Oxygen,
    7. Densities,   8. Molecules,   9. Carbon Dioxide,   10. Atmosphere (or air),
    11. Priestley,   12. Helium,   13. Natural,   14. Temperature,   15. Effervescence

B. *Gas Puzzler #1:* ethane; *Gas Puzzler #2:* methane

PS-15. CRYSTAL MATTER

1. a. salt,   b. amethyst,   c. pyrite,   d. rock candy
2. a. patterns,   b. amorphous,   c. cubic,   d. hexagonal,   e. edges
3. *Bonus Puzzler:* six

PS-16. PERIODIC TABLE OF ELEMENTS

A. 1. lithium,   2. Berkelium,   3. proton,   4. hydrogen,   5. Ba (Barium),   6. silver,
    7. family,   8. Bismuth,   9. Hafnium,   10. neutron,   11. chlorine,   12. silicon,
    13. electron,   14. fluorine,   15. shells,   16. Platinum,   17. Xenon,   18. Americium

B. 1. because there's never a charge with a neutron;   2. because she knew it would
    be a "stable" relationship

C. Indium (In) + Potassium (K) = KIn or kin; Silver (Ag) + Nitrogen (N) = NAg or nag;
    Protactinium (Pa) + Indium (In) = PaIn or pain; Americium (Am) + Chlorine (Cl) =
    ClAm or clam

PS-17. ATOMS

1. millions of atoms from the black mineral, graphite (pencil lead)
2. NaCl or sodium chloride, common table salt
3. a. matter,   b. nucleus,   c. electrons,   d. proton,   e. quark,   f. space

PS-18. ELEMENTS EVERYWHERE

1. matter, substance, cannot, separated, similar, substance;   a. iron, b. tin
2. Letters c, o, a, r, n, and b = coarnb; unscrambled they spell carbon. Other clues:
    diamond, symbol C, pencil lead (graphite), coke, and charcoal—all are related to
    the element carbon
3. a. I (Iodine),   b. At (Astatine),   c. Au (Gold),   d. Ne (Neon),   e. Hg (Mercury),
    f. Zn (Zinc)
4. in ELEMENTary school

PS-19. CHEMICAL SYMBOLS

1. a. Ru, b. F, c. V, d. Sb, e. Pb, f. Hg, g. Se, h. Y, i. Ac, j. Ag, k. K, l. S
2. tahcmsnLilaetsi; a. alchemists; b. Latin
3. a. No, because both first and last names are capitalized;   b. one, Sr (Strontium)

PS–20. EIGHT MYSTERY ELEMENTS

A. 1. Ca (calcium),   2. Ni (nickel),   3. C (carbon),   4. Ce (cerium),   5. N (nitrogen),
    6. Pb (lead),   7. S (sulfur),   8. P (phosphorus)
B. (*any order*) Ne (neon), Te (tellurium), N (nitrogen), Tl (thallium), Mn (manganese),
    Tm (thulium)

PS–21. ELEMENT RHYMERS

1. boron (B), 2. neon (Ne), 3. zinc (Zn), 4. Iodine (I), 5. cobalt (Co), 6. copper (Cu),
7. lead (Pb), 8. chlorine (Cl), 9. fluorine (F), 10. bromine (Br), 11. gold (Au),
12. molybdenum (Mo), 13. nickel (Ni), 14. manganese (Mn), 15. tin (Sn), 16. arsenic (As),
17. krypton (Kr), 18. sulfur (S), 19. antimony (Sb), 20. phosphorus (P)

PS–22. HYDROGEN

A. 1. acids (ac,ids),   2. active (ac,tive),   3. oxygen (oxy,gen),   4. natural (nat,ur,al),
    5. tritium (tri,ti,um),   6. metals (met,als),   7. splint (sp,li,nt),   8. electron (elect,ron),
    9. density (den,sity),   10. readily (read,ily),   11. ammonia (am,mon,ia),
    12. twice (tw,ice),   13. water (wa,ter),   14. universe (uni,ver,se)
B. because it doesn't have any "taste"

PS–23. OXYGEN

1. rocks, dioxide, Priestley, eight, water, electrons, oxides, monoxide, symbol, energy,
    life, protons, ozone, mixture, photosynthesis, hydrogen, molecule, burning
2. (*Possible answers include*)
    elements—eel, men, stem;   compounds—cod, pods (seed), mom, scum;
    chemistry—tree, sister, mice, rice;   reaction—rat, cat, otter, raccoon

PS–24. CARBON

1. True: b, c, e, f, h, i, j, k, m, n, o, r
2. c. 12
3. a. bones,   b. car,   c. banana,   d. ear,   e. bear

PS–25. HYDROCARBONS

1. methane (CH_4) and butane ($C_4 H_{10}$); a. There would be no change. The extra H
    would be surplus; b. You would have enough carbon atoms for hexane, $C_6 H_{14}$).
2.

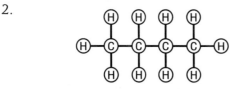

$C_4 H_{10}$ butane (gas)

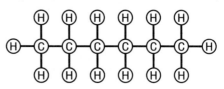

$C_6 H_{14}$ hexane (liquid)

PS-26. METAL MATTER

1. a. 3, b. 4, c. 2, d. 4, e. 2, f. 4, g. 3, h. 3, i. 1, j. 4, k. 2, l. 3, m. 1, n. 2, o. 1
2. One way is by crossing out the CO_3; or use a pencil to write $ZnCO_3$ on paper, then erase the CO_3.

PS-27. ALKALI METALS

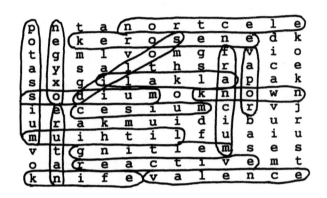

1. electron;   2. potassium;   3. sodium;   4. solid;   5. alkali;   6. Francium;
7. Lithium;   8. kerosene, oxygen, vapor;   9. known;   10. melting;   11. reactive, valence;
12. knife;   13. nature;   14. cesium

PS-28. METALLOIDS

A. 1. boron,   2. silicon,   3. antimony,   4. germanium,   5. arsenic,   6. tellurium
B. zigzag
C. A metalloid is an element that has properties BETWEEN metals and nonmetals.

PS-29. HALOGENS

A. 1. Fluorine (F): a,d,g,l,n,q,r,t;   2. Chlorine (Cl): a,d,e,g,j,k,m,n,q,s;
    3. Bromine (Br): a,f,g,i,j,n,p,q;   4. Iodine (I): a,b,c,g,j,n,o,q,u,v;
    5. Astatine (At): a,b,g,h,n,q
B. "It" turned out to be a "BrAt" (brat).

PS-30. NOBLE OR INERT GASES

1. a. Argon (3),   b. Neon (2),   c. Xenon (5),   d. Krypton (4)—2000 pounds = ton,
   e. Helium (1),   f. Radon (6)
2. Rearrange the letters in INERT to spell NITER.

PS-31. CHEMISTRY TERM PUZZLE

1. catalyst, 2. compound, 3. halides, 4. hydrolosis, 5. electron, 6. evaporation,
7. metabolism, 8. mole, 9. inert, 10. isotope, 11. solution, 12. salt,
13. temperature, 14. titanium, 15. reagent, 16. residue, 17. yttrium, 18. yeast

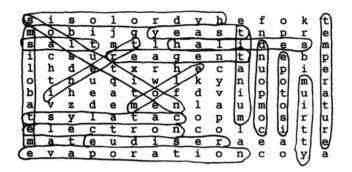

PS-32. ENERGY

A. 1. reaction, 2. photovoltaic, 3. chemical, 4. temperature, 5. electricity,
    6. solar, 7. potential, 8. kinetic, 9. catalyst, 10. endothermic, 11. engine,
    12. turbine, 13. gasoline, 14. bonding, 15. combustion, 16. nuclear,
    17. water, 18. mechanical, 19. electromagnetic, 20. geothermal

B. 12, 20, 6, 16, 4, 17, 15, 8; NOTE: 98

C. 1. ignition, magneto; 2. tiger, nit

PS-33. NUCLEAR ENERGY

1. Nuclear reactions take place in the sun; 2. Nuclear fission occurs when a nucleus
breaks into two or more nuclei; 3. During fusion, two nuclei collide and release
enormous energy; 4. A chain reaction is a series of repeated reactions that occur
very rapidly; 5. A chain reaction begins when the nucleus of a uranium atom is
bombarded with a neutron; 6. As neighboring uranium nuclei split, huge quantities
of energy are released, 7. Nuclear energy can be used to produce electricity;
8. Electricity is produced from nuclear energy in nuclear reactors; 9. The steam in
nuclear reactors turns turbines and generates electricity.

PS-34. GEOTHERMAL ENERGY

1. wells	8. centigrade
2. Iceland	9. renewable
3. heat	10. environment
4. cook	11. steam
5. geyser	12. crust
6. earth	13. decay
7. active	14. thin

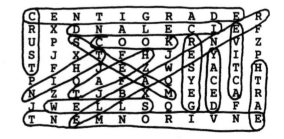

PS–35. PHYSICAL CHANGE

1. bending
    crumpling
    crushing
    dissolving
    freezing
    mangling
    melting
    stretching
    tearing
    twisting

2. SNAP

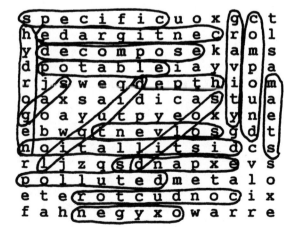

PS–36. CHEMICAL CHANGE

1. (*Possible answers*) a. explodes, b. carbon, c. sour milk, d. humus (or soil), e. rust (or iron oxide), f. rotten, g. charcoal, h. ash, i. chyme (or nutrients)

2. photosynthesis

3. (a) energy, (b) heat, (c) light, (d) sound.

PS–37. COMPOUND WATER

A. 1. solid, liquid, gas;   2. expands;   3. solvent, decompose;   4. potable;
    5. polluted;   6. distillation;   7. depth;   8. hydrogen, oxygen;   9. conductor;
    10. compound;   11. specific gravity;   12. centigrade;   13. steam

B. hard water or hard H_2O, and soft water or soft H_2O

PS-38. COMPOUND MAZE

A. 1. carbon dioxide
    2. sugar
    3. water
    4. baking soda
    5. methane
    6. sand
    7. salt
    8. ammonia
    9. butane
    10. rust

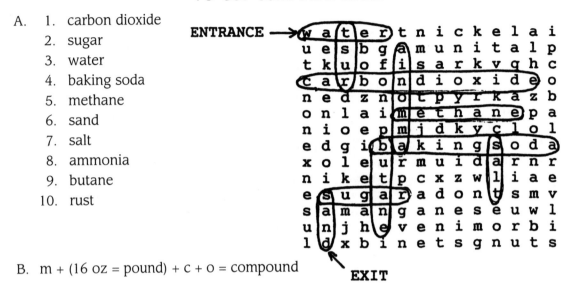

B. m + (16 oz = pound) + c + o = compound

PS-39. SOLUTIONS

1. a. water + salt; b. water + sugar; c. water + chlorine tablets; d. water + Alka Seltzer
2. **ACROSS:** 3. suspension, 4. saturated, 6. substance, 7. sugar, 8. soluble, 10. solvent; **DOWN:** 1. solute, 2. separate, 5. shake, 6. solution, 8. salt, 9. settle

PS-40. ACIDS AND BASES

1. ACID: Acids taste sour and sharp. Student drawings will vary. Blue litmus turns red. BASE: Bases taste bitter. Red litmus turns blue.
2. True: a, c, f, g
3. A, A, B, A, A, A, B, B
4. BASEball

PS-41. SCRAMBLED FACTS ABOUT FORCES

A. 1. Work equals force times distance;   2. Frictional force slows down moving objects;   3. Balanced forces are equal in size and opposite in direction; 4. A net force on an object always changes the velocity of the object; 5. Newton's three laws of motion describe the effect of forces;   6. The weight of an object is the measure of the force of gravity;   7. All forces are pushes or pulls; 8. Electromagnetic forces hold atoms and molecules together;   9. Buoyancy is a force that pushes up on objects when they are placed in a fluid;   10. Force acting upon a unit area of surface is called pressure.

B. momentum; the letters that spell "mom" represent 37.5 percent of the word momentum

PS–42. FOUR-LETTER FORCES PUZZLE

A. 1. centripetal, 2. centrifugal, 3. (across) g force, 3. (down) gravitational,
   4. amps, 5. lifting, 6. thrust, 7. torque, 8. vector, 9. (across, backwards) electric,
   9. (down, backwards) magnetic, 10. energize, 11. motorize

B. OXEN (draft refers to drawing or pulling loads)

PS–43. TIME FOR WORK

A. 1. force, 2. energy, 3. work, 4. newton, 5. meter, 6. machines, 7. input,
   8. power, 9. joule, 10. watts

B. 1. Mary did more work. She was moving a force (object) through a distance.
   2. Yes. You're providing force to drive an object through the air.
   3. An object is moving through a distance:

diosbtjaenccte

PS–44. MACHINES, PART 1

Puzzle One: (Across) 1. broom, 3. force; (Down) 1. brittle, 2. fulcrum
Puzzle Two: (Across) 4. third, 6. screw; (Down) 4. tongs, 5. world
Puzzle Three: (Across) 7. compound machine, 9. first class lever;
                (Down) 7. crowbar, 8. ferrule
Puzzle Four: (Across) 10. mechanical, 12. resistance; (Down) 10. moose, 11. lever

PS–45. MACHINES, PART 2

A.
1. input	11. ideal
2. effort	12. speed
3. first	13. lever
4. wedge	14. direction
5. fulcrum	15. pulleys
6. compound	16. hammer
7. friction	17. second
8. resistance	18. force
9. efficiency	19. output
10. third	20. power

```
p o u n d z b s v e
t i o n e e d i e c
p e c r u m f s r t
u a h d i r d t i i
t l j g r c e a e o
o k m e r q z n n n
r o n d p u t c c f
t r s t k l l e y s
b f h j w e r q x b
```

B. 16. e, 15. g, 4. h, 18. a, 8. b, 1. f, 20. d, 13. c

PS–46. NEWTON'S FIRST LAW OF MOTION

1. i (eye) + n + a + e + t (tee) + i + r = inertia

2. Sketches will vary. This is an example of Newton's first law because a moving object (car) tends to keep going in the same direction.

3. a. metal bat (tablatem)
    b. racket (diagonal)
    c. linebacker (rekcabenil)
    d. dart board
    e. paddle (elddap)

4. Fig Newton

r	e	k	c	a	b	e	n	i	l
d	a	r	t	b	o	a	r	d	s
w	v	c	l	p	q	n	u	k	z
i	y	j	k	i	c	b	t	w	m
a	i	t	g	e	l	d	d	a	p
t	a	b	l	a	t	e	m	x	o

PS–47. NEWTON'S SECOND LAW OF MOTION

1. a. Circle all items; b. Circle all items except vacuum; c. Circle all items except "molecules at -273 degrees C" because scientists believe all molecular movement ceases at this temperature.

2. 63.75 N (0.75 kg × 85 m = 63.75 N)

3. The force is a push or pull.

4. MASSachusetts

PS–48. NEWTON'S THIRD LAW OF MOTION

1. a. ACTION: Feet push against the cement, REACTION: The cement pushes against the feet; b. ACTION: The oars push on the water, REACTION: The water pushes on the oars; c. ACTION: The gases escape from the rocket, REACTION: The rocket accelerates off the launching pad.

2.

s	h	c	d	e	o	b
k	i	q	m	c	a	v
a	r	i	f	l	e	m
t	g	x	g	y	l	
e	p	o	r	t	a	l
u	o	s	u	k	v	a
o	w	c	z	d	h	b

3. C + C + C + C = FORCES (4 C's)

4. In the middle of his last name: Ne"wt"on; wt, of course, is the abbreviation for weight.

PS–49. HEAT

1. solids, 2. energy, 3. radiation, 4. calorie, 5. kinetic, 6. convection, 7. insulator,
8. engine, 9. turbine, 10. fusion, 11. temperature, 12. reaction, 13. expand

PS–50. PHYSICAL SCIENCE PUZZLERS

1. cheater, wheat, theater
2. Rearrange the last four letters in CRYSTAL—STAL—to spell SALT; compound: sodium chloride
3. In the first five letters of pressure: press
4. 1 + 2 + 3 + 2 = 8 (eight). The 23rd letter of the English alphabet is w.
   W + eight = Weight, the gravitational force that Earth exerts on an object.
5. *As* is the chemical symbol for arsenic (poison), so U (you) would probably die from arsenic poisoning.
6. (*Possible answer*)   ~~non~~metal (eliminate the non)
7. (*Possible answer*)   m S a P t A t C e E r
8. (*Possible answer*)

$$\begin{array}{c}\text{m}\\ \text{C O B A L T}\\ \text{g}\\ \text{I R O N}\\ \text{N I C K E L}\\ \text{t}\end{array}$$

9. (*Possible answer*)

$$\begin{array}{l}\text{W—LOW PRESSURE}\\ \text{A}\\ \text{T}\\ \text{E}\\ \text{R—HIGH PRESSURE}\end{array}$$

10. (*Possible answer*)

sound

PS–51. ELECTRICITY

1. c, g, f, e, h, d, a, b
2. The particles (charges) in Figure B are unlike. Unlike charges attract.
3. Neutral; The object is a plus (+) sign. There are four negative charges and four positive charges.
4. The lamps ran out of electricity (electr. . . . .).
5. a "short" circuit

PS–52. MAGNETISM

1.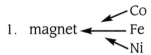

2. (*Possible answer*) Use the magnets as a lifting device to lift the wood.
3. a. F,   b. T,   c. T,   d. F,   e. F,   f. F,   g. T,   h. T
4. a magnet
5. He felt it would give him "animal magnetism."

PS-53. SOUND

1.

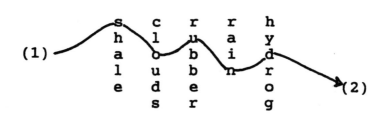

2. a. power mower,   b. rock music,   c. hungry baby,   d. jet engine,
   e. chain saw,   f. ambulance siren

3. baa, whinny, hiss, purr, woof, caw, chirp

4. $\dfrac{\text{water}}{\text{sound}}$ (sound under water)

5. Sound can't travel on the moon. The moon has no air.

PS-54. LIGHT

1. a. shadow, b. eclipse, c. mirror, d. telescope, e. refraction, f. mirage, g. spectrum

2. Light cannot travel around corners.

3. 8.3 seconds

4. (*Possible answer*) Draw a line under OHIO. The line will appear on top of OHIO in the mirror.

5. coins, people, paper, quarters, vaults, pennies

6. Adjust the knob on the bathroom scale.

PS-55. LIGHT: REFLECTION, PART 1

A. 1. 62 degrees   3. 47 degrees
   2. 23 degrees   4. 12 degrees

B. 1. waxed gym floor
   2. calm clear lake

PS-56. LIGHT: REFLECTION, PART 2

A. Students should show the angle of reflection equal to the angle of incidence.

B. If students make their drawings in accordance with the law of reflection, the reflected ray should bounce off all three mirrors.

PS-57. LIGHT: REFRACTION

1. glass
2. air
3. lenses
4. bent

5. spectrum
6. red
7. prism
8. violet

9. camera
10. index
11. vacuum
12. diamond

PS-58. COLOR

1. a. reflect,   b. complementary,   c. cones,   d. spectrum,   e. pigment,   f. white,
   g. hue,   h. shade,   i. tone,   j. absorbed,   k. red,   l. violet,   m. frequency
2. (*Possible answers*) red, orange, blue, violet, black, purple, green, pink

PS-59. PHYSICAL SCIENCE MINI-PROBLEMS

1. Accuracy counts because you want to be *sure* (meaSURE).
2. The remaining three letters are UFN. Unscramble them and you'll see that the activity should have been FUN.
3. a. ant,   b. gnat,   c. crane fly
4. a. den + sity = density; hard + ness = hardness; col + or = color
5. pineapple, date, banana, apricot, melon, pear, passion (fruit), tomato, raspberries
6. kinetic energy.

PS-60. MORE PHYSICAL SCIENCE MINI-PROBLEMS

1. She wrote the word TEMPERATURE on the board. Then she measured the length of the word in centimeters.
2. (*Possible answer*) Hang a thermometer from the patio roof or front door. Then you can measure (take) the temperature in the front or back yards.
3. Francium + Iodine + Carbon + Titanium + Oxygen + Nitrogen =
   Fr + I + C + Ti + O + N or friction
4. B R U = R U B

   This arrangement produces a RUB; hence, RUB produces friction.
5. a. tea,   b. hen,   c. rat
6. (*Possible answers*) inertia, friction, reaction, projectile, kinetic, potential